T0260169

Early praise for *Build Location-Based Projects for iOS*

This book is for every iOS developer who wants to dive deeper into location-based technologies by working on real-world projects using practical examples. I'd highly recommend it to any aspiring iOS developer.

➤ **Marcus Kida**
  CEO, Bearologics UG

This book takes a hands-on approach to Apple's CoreLocation framework, explaining its core features using actual projects built in different technologies. You'll get to use programmatic layouts, storyboards, and even some SwiftUI. And, of course, you will learn how to make good use of location services on iOS to build rich apps for your users. Really well written.

➤ **Donny Wals**

This book not only gets you amazingly up to date with all the great ways of using location and the various hardware related to movement in iOS, it is also a great way of seeing the three different approaches of building user interfaces: Storyboard, UIKit in Code, or SwiftUI. You won't regret buying this book; you might even buy one for a friend!

➤ **Manuel Carrasco Molina**
  Apple Technologist

Nothing less than thrilling examples, a playful deep dive into core iOS programming, and an insight into various techniques of building apps. Pure fun to read and learn.

➤ **Klaus Rodewig**
  Founder and Hacker, Appnö UG

Build Location-Based Projects for iOS

GPS, Sensors, and Maps

Dominik Hauser

The Pragmatic Bookshelf

Raleigh, North Carolina

Many of the designations used by manufacturers and sellers to distinguish their products are claimed as trademarks. Where those designations appear in this book, and The Pragmatic Programmers, LLC was aware of a trademark claim, the designations have been printed in initial capital letters or in all capitals. The Pragmatic Starter Kit, The Pragmatic Programmer, Pragmatic Programming, Pragmatic Bookshelf, PragProg and the linking *g* device are trademarks of The Pragmatic Programmers, LLC.

Every precaution was taken in the preparation of this book. However, the publisher assumes no responsibility for errors or omissions, or for damages that may result from the use of information (including program listings) contained herein.

Our Pragmatic books, screencasts, and audio books can help you and your team create better software and have more fun. Visit us at *https://pragprog.com*.

The team that produced this book includes:

Publisher: Andy Hunt
VP of Operations: Janet Furlow
Executive Editor: Dave Rankin
Copy Editor: Rachel Monaghan
Layout: Gilson Graphics

For sales, volume licensing, and support, please contact *support@pragprog.com*.

For international rights, please contact *rights@pragprog.com*.

ISBN-13: 978-1-68050-781-2
Book version: P1.0—August 2020

Contents

Acknowledgments

Everyone at the Pragmatic Bookshelf, thank you for helping me write this book. I dreamed about this for a very long time, and now it's true. I'm so happy and proud.

Thank you, Adaobi Obi Tulton, for all your help and great suggestions. The book is so much better because of it, and it was a blast to work on this with you.

Thank you, Dave Thomas and Andy Hunt, for making me a better programmer and for creating The Pragmatic Bookshelf. I am very grateful to be part of it.

A big thank you to my technical editors, Manuel Carrasco Molina, Scott Davis, Jeff Kelley, Marcus Kida, Kilian Koeltzsch, Nathan Mattes, Klaus M. Rodewig, Sven Schmidt, Jeremy Sydik, and Donny Wals. Without you the book would not be half as good. Especially, thank you, Jeremy Sydik, for pointing out some major flaws in the first draft.

Thank you, Isa. You are the best wife on earth! Thank you for tolerating me during this time (and in general). I'm sorry that I often didn't listen properly because I was thinking about the book. Thank you, my two children, for your patience when I was busy writing just one more sentence.

Introduction

Learning new skills works best when it's fun. You dive deeper and deeper. Hours pass and you can't stop reading and experimenting.

But there's also the outside world. And there's the feeling you have after a nice walk in the woods. Wouldn't it be cool if you could combine learning about iOS development with being outside?

This book features four inspiring projects you get to test outside. You'll draw on a map by moving in the real world, measure the length of a swing while swinging, measure how long someone's outside, and share augmented reality views. As we build these projects, we'll also be looking at the three main approaches to constructing user interfaces: storyboards, code, and SwiftUI.

Who This Book Is For

This book is for developers who already have rudimentary experience with iOS development and want to learn about GPS, sensors, and ARKit. And even if you already have experience with location-based tools, the projects in this book might give you new ideas for your own apps.

I assume that you already have Xcode installed and know the basics about its structure. If you have worked through a beginner's book or other beginner resources, you are perfectly prepared to work through the projects in this book. The first three chapters, in particular, cover in detail what you have to do in Xcode to follow along.

Who Am I?

My name is Dominik Hauser. After I finished my PhD in physics, I worked at a university as a tutor and as such was looking for an app about physics and math formulas. It was the beginning of the App Store, and the only apps I could find didn't fit my needs. So I decided to build my own. Two years later I switched careers to become a full-time iOS developer, and I haven't looked back since then.

What I like most about iOS development is when someone finds a cool way to use the available resources to create something nobody has seen before. One of these moments was the invention of the pull-to-refresh control by Loren Brichter in the early days of iOS. The users loved this kind of user interaction, and Apple added it to iOS some years later.

For me iOS still has lots of corners where discoveries can be made. You need to keep your eyes and your mind open, and you need to experiment and explore. Let your mind wander sometimes and try ideas that seem silly.

One day while riding my bike home after work, I had just such an idea: a pull-to-refresh control that's also a break-out game played by scrolling the table view. A few months later I implemented it and posted it to GitHub, a site to share open source projects. I think (and hope) no one ever put that into a real app because it really was silly, but nevertheless, it received more than 2,000 stars.

The projects in this book are meant to be a starting point for your own experiments. I hope while working through the chapters you get ideas for how to create something special and unique from the example apps. Explore, try ideas even if they seem strange or too big, and, most importantly, have fun!

What This Book Covers

To maximize what you learn and to keep the content of the book interesting, we'll use three different approaches for the user interface in this book. In two chapters we build the user interface using a storyboard. We also build user interfaces in code and using SwiftUI. A good iOS developer should be able to choose the best user interface framework for the problem at hand, and learning the three major approaches will make you a better developer.

Chapter 1: Drawing on Maps

> In this chapter we build an app that lets us draw on a map by moving around in the real world. We add overlays to maps and fetch the device's location from the GPS sensors. Finally, we share the resulting image on social media.

> The user interface in this project is created in code.

Chapter 2: Measuring Length with Gravitation

> We use the accelerometer built into the iPhone to measure the period of a swing. We draw the data onto the screen using Core Graphics.

> The user interface in this project is created using a storyboard.

Chapter 3: Automating with Geofences

In this chapter we build an app that allows us to set a geofence. Whenever the iPhone enters or exits the geofence, our app stores the time. We use this data to calculate how long the user has been outside of this geofence each day.

The user interface in this project is created using SwiftUI.

Chapter 4: Sharing Augmented Reality

In this chapter we build an app that allows us to draw a virtual text for other app users to find. We use ARKit and SpriteKit to render the text into the augmented reality view.

The user interface in this project is created using a storyboard.

Free Developer Account

 You don't need a paid Apple Developer account to work though this book. But Apple restricts the number of apps you can install on your device to three for the free developer account. You can build and run apps on the iOS simulator that comes with Xcode without any restrictions. If you have a free account, I suggest you select the three apps you would like to test on your real iOS device before you start working through each chapter. Keep in mind that the simulator cannot simulate motion events.

In addition, with a free account the apps work only for seven days before you have to deploy them again onto the device using Xcode.

How to Read This Book

The chapters are independent from one another. But if you're new to iOS development in general, you should read the book from cover to cover. The first two chapters explain in detail what to do and why to do it that way, and the last two chapters assume you've read or already understand those explanations.

As I mentioned, throughout the book we use storyboards, code, and SwiftUI to create the user interfaces for the apps. When you have finished the book you can increase your skills and maximize your learning by recreating the projects using a different approach for the user interface. Or you can even build an app that combines two or three of the projects. Invent something new.

Creating with Swift

The code in this book is written in Swift, which is the de facto standard for iOS apps these days. It's a powerful language that's easy for beginners to learn.

I assume that you have a basic knowledge of Swift and that you already have created some simple iOS projects with it. If you need to refresh your Swift knowledge, you can download *The Swift Programming Language* for free from the official Swift website.[1]

If you don't understand some of the code in this book, search *The Swift Programming Language* or go to Stack Overflow[2] to get answers.

Online Resources

This book has a website where you will find links to source code and errata.[3] You are free to use the source code in your own applications as you see fit.

If you purchased the ebook, you can click the gray box above the code extracts to directly download the extract.

Let's have fun!

---

1. www.apple.com/swift/
2. stackoverflow.com
3. https://pragprog.com/titles/dhios/

CHAPTER 1

Drawing on Maps

Have you ever watched a child draw? Most children love drawing and are proud of their results.

When they grow up, however, most people stop drawing. Often it's because they try to draw photorealistic pictures, or they try to create something as appealing as the great artists' masterpieces, and they fail. Or they think drawing needs a purpose to be valuable, like being useful for their job. What a pity.

We should search for opportunities to have fun again without judging the result. This chapter is one of those opportunities. We'll build an app that draws on the map as we walk around in the real world. The resulting pictures probably won't win any awards, but the act of drawing will be fun. We'll also see how to add overlays to maps in iOS and how to share the resulting pictures with friends and family.

Apps use overlays on maps to add or emphasize valuable information. After you have worked through this chapter, you'll be able to use map overlays in your own apps.

We'll define the user interface of this app in code files. The result will look like the image on page 2.

Creating the Xcode Project

Open Xcode and create a new project with the keyboard shortcut ⌘⇧N. Choose the Single View App template and click Next. For the Product Name, type Walk2Draw; select Storyboard from the User Interface drop-down menu; and deselect the check marks for Use Core Data, Include Unit Tests, and Include UI Tests. Click Next, choose a location in the file system, and click Create.

In Appendix 1, Debugging on the Go, on page 119, we'll build a small library to add on-the-go logging to our apps. You can work through the appendix

now if you'd like, or you can do it later and use the library I have prepared for you. This library allows us to see what the app is doing under the hood while we're outside drawing.

You need to add your GitHub account in your Xcode preferences to be able to add the prepared package to the project. If you don't have a GitHub account, you can download the package from GitHub and use a file URL from your Mac.

In Xcode, select File > Swift Packages > Add Package Dependency. Xcode presents a pop-up window for the selection of the package. Enter the URL https://github.com/ dasdom/LogStore2.git in the search field and hit return. (If you've worked through the appendix, you can use the URL of your own Swift package.)

Select the package from the list and click Next. In the next pop-up window, we can select the version we want to use. Depending on how much you worked on the exercises, the version is something like 1.0.x and it's set to use all versions Up to Next Major. The selection window should look like the image on page 3, which shows exactly what the settings should be. Click Next.

A new pop-up window appears, asking us to which target Xcode should add the package. We have only one target, so we don't have to change anything here. Click Finish to add the package to the project.

Now that you've seen how to add Swift packages to projects, let's look at how to activate the LogStore library. This library displays the log when we knock the left side of our phone against our left palm. To activate this gesture, we need to add a log trigger using the existing window. Open SceneDelegate.swift in Xcode and import LogStore below the existing import statements:

Map/Walk2Draw/Walk2Draw/SceneDelegate.swift

```
import UIKit
import LogStore
```

Then add the highlighted lines in the following code to SceneDelegate:

Map/Walk2Draw/Walk2Draw/SceneDelegate.swift

```
class SceneDelegate: UIResponder, UIWindowSceneDelegate {

    var window: UIWindow?
    var trigger: LogTrigger?

    func scene(_ scene: UIScene,
               willConnectTo session: UISceneSession,
               options connectionOptions: UIScene.ConnectionOptions) {

        guard let _ = (scene as? UIWindowScene) else { return }

        #if DEBUG
        trigger = LogTrigger(in: window)
        #endif
    }
    // ...
    // other methods
    // ...
}
```

With this code we add a property for the log trigger and initialize it in scene(_:willConnectTo:options:) with the window property. This is all we have to do to set up the LogStore library.

Note that we put that code between #if DEBUG and #endif statements to make sure that we don't accidentally ship a version with the debug gesture activated.

With the logging library now set up, we can proceed with our drawing app.

Removing the Storyboard

The user interface of the app we're going to build is quite simple. This is a good opportunity to practice building apps without storyboards. In the next chapter we'll use storyboards again.

Pro Tip: Always Practice

A good developer can build apps with storyboards, with XIBs, in code, and with SwiftUI. You should practice your abilities in all these different approaches. Only when you are proficient in each approach can you decide which is best for the project at hand.

When setting up a new app with Xcode, you can choose only between storyboard and SwiftUI for building the user interface. If you want to build the user interface in code instead, you have to choose one of the two options and then remove the files and settings you don't need. What you choose mainly depends on your preferences. The amount of work to remove the storyboard is comparable to that for removing SwiftUI support.

The first entry in the project navigator, with the blue icon and the name Walk2Draw, is the project itself. Click it to open the project settings. Next, select the target in the TARGETS section to open the target settings. Select the General tab if it's not already selected. Xcode defines the initial storyboard of an app in the section Deployment Info, next to Main Interface. Remove *Main* from the text field to tell Xcode that the app shouldn't load a storyboard when it launches.

As of Xcode 11, the storyboard is defined in a second place, so we'll have to make changes there as well. Open the file Info.plist and navigate to Application Scene Manifest > Scene Configuration > Application Session Role > Item 0. Delete the whole line with the setting for Storyboard Name. The result should look like what's shown in the image on page 5.

Once we've made the changes, the storyboard won't be used anymore, so we can delete it. Select the file Main.storyboard and remove it from the project by deleting it.

If you think removing a storyboard from a project should be easier, I feel you. I hope Apple adds the option to use neither a storyboard nor SwiftUI in a future version of Xcode, but I won't hold my breath.

Now that the storyboard is gone, we need to create the window and assign its rootViewController when the app loads. Open SceneDelegate.swift, look for the

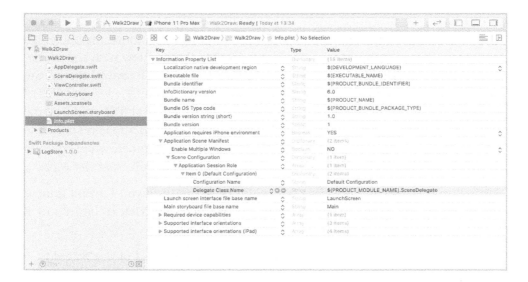

method scene(_:willConnectTo:options:), and replace the underscore (which acts as a placeholder) in the following line of code with scene:

Map/Walk2Draw/Walk2Draw/SceneDelegate.swift

```
guard let _ = (scene as? UIWindowScene) else { return }
```

Afterward, the line should look like this:

Map/Walk2Draw/Walk2Draw/SceneDelegate.swift

```
guard let scene = (scene as? UIWindowScene) else { return }
```

With this line we try to cast the scene variable passed into scene(_:willConnect-To:options:) to the type UIWindowScene. If it fails, we return from this method. Now change the contents of scene(_:willConnectTo:options:) so that it looks like the following code. The changed lines are highlighted.

Map/Walk2Draw/Walk2Draw/SceneDelegate.swift

```
func scene(_ scene: UIScene,
           willConnectTo session: UISceneSession,
           options connectionOptions: UIScene.ConnectionOptions) {

  guard let scene = (scene as? UIWindowScene) else { return }

  window = UIWindow(windowScene: scene)
  window?.rootViewController = ViewController()
  window?.makeKeyAndVisible()

  #if DEBUG
  trigger = LogTrigger(in: window)
  #endif
}
```

In this code, we first instantiate a new instance of UIWindow using the scene. As of iOS 13, a scene represents the user interface—or more precisely, an instance of the user interface. If we don't provide the window with the scene, the screen remains black. Next we assign an instance of ViewController to the rootViewController property of the window to define the initial view controller of our app. Then we call makeKeyAndVisible() to tell the window that it should become visible and that it is the *key window*. The key window of an app is responsible for handling nontouch and keyboard-related events. Remember, when creating the window of the application in code, we always have to call makeKeyAndVisible().

Setting up the user interface in code might be something you haven't done a lot. Let's see if our changes work. We can use an easy trick to figure out if Xcode launched the correct view controller.

Open ViewController.swift and add the following line at the end of viewDidLoad():

```
Map/Walk2Draw/Walk2Draw/ViewController.swift
view.backgroundColor = .red
```

Select your favorite simulator and build and run the code by clicking the play button in Xcode. After the app is loaded, you should see a red screen in the simulator. If you don't, retrace your steps and compare them with your code and settings.

Pro Tip: Alternate Simulators

 Alternate the simulators you use during development to find user-interface bugs or layout problems related to false assumptions as early as possible.

Managing Location Services

The location of a user's device is sensitive information, and that's why our app needs to get permission from users to access it. In this section, we'll create a class that manages the access to and handling of the location data.

In Xcode, create a new file using the shortcut ⌘N, select the Cocoa Touch Class template, and click Next. Type LocationProvider in the Class text field and make it a subclass of NSObject. Click Next and then click Create.

Asking for Permission

Our app will access the location services via an instance of CLLocationManager, which is defined in CoreLocation. Import CoreLocation below the existing import statement:

Map/Walk2Draw/Walk2Draw/LocationProvider.swift

```
import UIKit
import CoreLocation
```

This import statement makes the classes in the CoreLocation framework accessible in this file. Next, replace the LocationProvider class with the following code:

Map/Walk2Draw/Walk2Draw/LocationProvider.swift

```
class LocationProvider: NSObject, CLLocationManagerDelegate {

  private let locationManager: CLLocationManager

  override init() {
    locationManager = CLLocationManager()

    super.init()

    locationManager.delegate = self
    locationManager.distanceFilter = 1
    locationManager.requestWhenInUseAuthorization()
  }
}
```

This code adds a property for the location manager to LocationProvider and assigns it to a new instance of CLLocationManager in the initializer. As LocationProvider is a subclass of NSObject, we need to call super.init() before we can access the instance of LocationProvider via self. This is one of the rules of initialization in Swift. You can learn more about these rules in the official documentation provided by Apple.[1]

After the super.init() call, we assign self to the delegate property of the locationManager. The locationManager will notify its delegate about changes concerning the location services, such as when the authorization is changed or a new location is detected. Our LocationProvider class can act as the delegate of the location manager only when it conforms to the CLLocationManagerDelegate protocol. This is why we have added CLLocationManagerDelegate to the class declaration.

Next we set the distance filter to one meter, which means the locationManager will notify the delegate only when the device has moved at least that far. This is a good way to reduce the amount of data we have to deal with. Finally, we ask for permission to access the user's location when the app is in use.

Before we move on, let's import our LogStore library below the existing import statements:

---

1. https://docs.swift.org/swift-book/LanguageGuide/Initialization.html

Map/Walk2Draw/Walk2Draw/LocationProvider.swift

```
import UIKit
import CoreLocation
import LogStore
```

The locationManager notifies its delegate when the user has responded to the permission request. Add the following method to the end of LocationProvider:

Map/Walk2Draw/Walk2Draw/LocationProvider.swift

```
func locationManager(_ manager: CLLocationManager,
                     didChangeAuthorization status:
                     CLAuthorizationStatus) {
  switch status {
  case .authorizedWhenInUse:
    printLog("success")
  case .denied:
    printLog("denied")
    // you will implement this case
    // in the exercises
  default:
    break
  }
}
```

This code just prints the word success to the debug output if the user selects Allow in the authorization dialog. You will implement the other cases in the exercises for this chapter.

Before we move on with implementing LocationProvider, let's check whether asking for permission works. Add the highlighted lines in the following code to ViewController:

Map/Walk2Draw/Walk2Draw/ViewController.swift

```
class ViewController: UIViewController {

➤  var locationProvider: LocationProvider?

  override func viewDidLoad() {
    super.viewDidLoad()

    view.backgroundColor = .red

➤    locationProvider = LocationProvider()
  }
}
```

In this code we add a property of type LocationProvider to the view controller and initialize it in viewDidLoad(). This should trigger the authorization request as soon as the view of the view controller has loaded.

Build and run the app on the simulator. You won't see the authorization alert in the simulator. To figure out what's going on, open the debug console by selecting View > Debug Area > Activate Console. You should see something like this:

```
This app has attempted to access privacy-sensitive data without
a usage description. The app's Info.plist must contain an
"NSLocationWhenInUseUsageDescription" key with a string value
explaining to the user how the app uses this data
```

Errors with exact descriptions of what to do to fix them are the best! Let's do what the error suggests. Open the Info.plist and add an entry with the key NSLocationWhenInUseUsageDescription and the value "Your location is used to show your path on a map." When you're done, it should look like this:

▶ Supported interface orientations	◇	Array	(3 items)
▶ Supported interface orientations (iPad)	◇	Array	(4 items)
Privacy - Location When In Use Usage Description	◇ ⊕ ⊖	String	Your location is used to show your path on a map.

As you can see in the screenshot, Xcode does not show the key NSLocationWhenInUseUsageDescription but rather expands it to a more human-readable form: "Privacy - Location When In Use Usage Description."

Build and run the app again. After the app launches, iOS presents the location permission alert with three choices: Allow While Using App, Allow Once, and Don't Allow.

If the user selects Allow While Using App, our app can access the location of the device whenever it is running. If the user selects Allow Once, our app can access the location during this session and UIKit will ask for permission again the next time the app is launched. If the user selects Don't Allow, UIKit denies access to the device location.

Once a user has denied access to the location, the app can't ask again and the location manager always delivers the status denied. In this case, the app could show an alert that it cannot function properly and ask if the user wants to change the permission in the app settings. We could even redirect the user to the settings with the following code:

```
let settingsURL = URL(string: UIApplication.openSettingsURLString)!
UIApplication.shared.open(settingsURL)
```

In the running simulator, select Allow While Using App, and the word success gets printed to the debug console.

Pro Tip: Use a Real Description

Enter a real description of the app's usage right from the beginning. Even though you may be tempted to skip this step because you're eager to see the feature running, it's likely that you'll forget to improve the usage description before you submit the first version of the app to the App Store for review. Sit down for a few minutes and think about how users will feel when they read the description.

If you'd like to trigger the permission alert again during development, open the Settings app in the simulator, navigate to General > Reset, and select Reset Location & Privacy.

Toggle Tracking

To start tracking the user's location, we need to call startUpdatingLocation() on the locationManager. Add the following method in LocationProvider above the method locationManager(_:didChangeAuthorization:):

Map/Walk2Draw/Walk2Draw/LocationProvider.swift
```
func start() {
  locationManager.startUpdatingLocation()
}
```

This way, we abstract the locationManager away from the parts that are interested only in the location updates. Callers need to know only that they can start location updates, not who is going to deliver these updates.

Whenever there is an update for the location of the device, the locationManager calls the locationManager(_:didUpdateLocations:) of its delegate. To see this in action, add the following method to the end of LocationProvider:

Map/Walk2Draw/Walk2Draw/LocationProvider.swift
```
func locationManager(_ manager: CLLocationManager,
                     didUpdateLocations locations: [CLLocation]) {
  printLog("locations: \(locations)")
}
```

For testing purposes, we just print the locations delivered by the locationManager to the debug console. To start the tracking, add the following method to the class ViewController.

Map/Walk2Draw/Walk2Draw/ViewController.swift
```
override func viewWillAppear(_ animated: Bool) {
  super.viewWillAppear(animated)

  locationProvider?.start()
}
```

UIKit calls viewWillAppear(_:) when the view is about to be presented to the user. This is the perfect moment to start doing tasks like gathering location updates.

Build and run the app, and open the debug console. Then select the simulator menu item Features > Location > Custom Location... to simulate different locations. In the debug console you should see location updates pouring in when you change the simulated location. Great! We managed to track the user's movement.

If you don't see the location updates in the debug console, review the steps and compare them with the code you wrote.

The next step is to create the user interface.

Building the User Interface

The user interface of this app needs to be quite simple, as the app will be used while the user is walking around outside. It should be easy to use without requiring much thought.

The simplest user interface for the features we're trying to build has a map and three buttons: one to start and stop the tracking, one to clear the data, and one to share the drawing with friends and family. It will look like this:

Creating the View

Press ⌘N to add another Cocoa Touch Class to the project. Type the name DrawView in the Class text field and make it a subclass of UIView. Click Next and then click Create. Remove the comment inside the class.

In iOS, maps are usually presented to the user using the class MKMapView, which is defined in MapKit. Add an import statement for MapKit right below the existing import statement:

Map/Walk2Draw/Walk2Draw/DrawView.swift
```
import UIKit
import MapKit
```

Next we need four properties for the different user interface elements. Add the properties and the initializer shown in the following code to DrawView:

Map/Walk2Draw/Walk2Draw/DrawView.swift
```
import UIKit
import MapKit

class DrawView: UIView {

  let mapView: MKMapView
  let clearButton: UIButton
  let startStopButton: UIButton
  let shareButton: UIButton

  override init(frame: CGRect) {

    mapView = MKMapView()
    mapView.showsUserLocation = true

    clearButton = UIButton(type: .system)
    clearButton.setTitle("Clear", for: .normal)

    startStopButton = UIButton(type: .system)
    startStopButton.setTitle("Start", for: .normal)

    shareButton = UIButton(type: .system)
    shareButton.setTitle("Share", for: .normal)

    super.init(frame: frame)
  }
}
```

With mapView.showsUserLocation = true, we activate the blue circle on the map that shows the user's location. The buttons are plain, standard UIKit buttons. We use the type .system so that, by default, the buttons fade the title when they are tapped. For the other types, we would have to implement that behavior ourselves.

Because DrawView is a subclass of UIView, we also need to add an override for init?(coder:):

Map/Walk2Draw/Walk2Draw/DrawView.swift
```
required init?(coder: NSCoder) {
  fatalError("init(coder:) has not been implemented")
}
```

This initializer is required for all subclasses of UIView and UIViewController because UIKit calls this initializer when the views and view controller are loaded from a storyboard. As we're not using a storyboard for the user interface, we call fatalError() here to tell our future self that we didn't expect that view to be used in a storyboard.

You don't need to type this yourself; just wait until Xcode shows you the error. In the error message is a red stop sign with a white dot in the middle. Whenever you see one of those, you can click the stop sign, and Xcode will show you a *fix-it*. If you click the Fix button, Xcode will add the required initializer for you.

Pro Tip: Listen to Xcode

Whenever Xcode shows an error, read it and try to understand it. Search online for the error when you get stuck.

The better you are at understanding the errors and warnings Xcode presents to you, the more fun you'll have during development. Xcode is your friend.

Next we need to add some code to add the initialized subviews to the user interface. Add the highlighted lines in the following code to init(frame:):

Map/Walk2Draw/Walk2Draw/DrawView.swift
```
override init(frame: CGRect) {

    mapView = MKMapView()
    mapView.showsUserLocation = true

    clearButton = UIButton(type: .system)
    clearButton.setTitle("Clear", for: .normal)

    startStopButton = UIButton(type: .system)
    startStopButton.setTitle("Start", for: .normal)

    shareButton = UIButton(type: .system)
    shareButton.setTitle("Share", for: .normal)

    super.init(frame: frame)

    backgroundColor = .white

    let buttonStackView = UIStackView(
        arrangedSubviews: [clearButton, startStopButton, shareButton])
    buttonStackView.distribution = .fillEqually
```

```
➤    let stackView = UIStackView(
➤      arrangedSubviews: [mapView, buttonStackView])
➤    stackView.axis = .vertical
➤    addSubview(stackView)
    }
```

When defining the view of a view controller in code, always set the background color to an opaque color to avoid visual glitches in the default animation during presentation and dismissal. We set the background color to white because the default value is transparent (UIColor.clear).

Next we create a horizontal UIStackView with the three buttons and put that together with the map into a vertical UIStackView. Stack views arrange their content vertically or horizontally using only a few configuration options. As a result, they make it easy to build a simple user interface like the one we are creating here.

We add the second stack view as a subview to the view. We don't have to set the axis of the button stack view because .horizontal is the default value.

The only step left is the layout. Insert the highlighted lines in the following code to the end of init(frame:):

Map/Walk2Draw/Walk2Draw/DrawView.swift

```
override init(frame: CGRect) {

  // ...
  // setup of the map and the buttons
  // ...

  super.init(frame: frame)

  backgroundColor = .white

  let buttonStackView = UIStackView(
    arrangedSubviews: [clearButton, startStopButton, shareButton])
  buttonStackView.distribution = .fillEqually

  let stackView = UIStackView(
    arrangedSubviews: [mapView, buttonStackView])
  stackView.axis = .vertical
  addSubview(stackView)

➤  stackView.translatesAutoresizingMaskIntoConstraints = false
➤
➤  NSLayoutConstraint.activate([
➤    stackView.topAnchor.constraint(equalTo: topAnchor),
➤    stackView.leadingAnchor.constraint(equalTo: leadingAnchor),
➤    stackView.bottomAnchor.constraint(
➤      equalTo: safeAreaLayoutGuide.bottomAnchor),
➤    stackView.trailingAnchor.constraint(equalTo: trailingAnchor),
➤  ])

}
```

Before we activate the constraints for the stack view, we set translatesAutoresiz-ingMaskIntoConstraints to false to tell UIKit that we want to activate the needed constraints ourselves. Without this line, UIKit would activate constraints according to the auto-resizing mask of the stack view, which would conflict with our constraints. Our constraints pin the edges of the stack view to the edges of the view, except at the bottom. Because of the home indicator on the iPhone X and above, most of the time the bottom of a user interface should be pinned to the safe area guide.

Pro Tip: Activate All Constraints at Once

It is more performant to activate all constraints of a view at once instead of setting their isActive property to true individually. NSLayout-Constraint provides the class method activate(_:) for this task. The argument is an array of constraints.

Activating a constraint is like adding it in Interface Builder.

In the next section we'll build the view controller for our user interface.

Creating the View Controller

Create a new file with ⌘N, choose the Cocoa Touch Class template, and click Next. Type the name DrawViewController in the Class text field and make it a subclass of UIViewController. Make sure the check box for "Also create XIB file" is not selected. Click Next and then click Create. Replace the contents of the class with the following code:

```
Map/Walk2Draw/Walk2Draw/DrawViewController.swift
override func loadView() {
  let contentView = DrawView(frame: .zero)

  view = contentView
}
```

We create an instance of DrawingView with a frame of zero. It doesn't matter which frame we use for the view because the view's size and position are defined by the view controller. We assign the instance to the view property of the view controller. You need to do this in loadView() because UIKit calls this method, and if it isn't defined in a view controller, it assigns a blank view to the view property.

This is all the code we need to set up the loading of the view without using Interface Builder. To check if this works, open SceneDelegate and replace the line

```
Map/Walk2Draw/Walk2Draw/SceneDelegate.swift
window?.rootViewController = ViewController()
```

with

Map/Walk2Draw/Walk2Draw/SceneDelegate.swift
```
window?.rootViewController = DrawViewController()
```

Build and run the app on the simulator. You should see a map like the one in the following image. It works! At least, the user interface does.

Now delete ViewController.swift, as we don't need it anymore.

To be able to present the path on the map, we need to pass the locations from the locationProvider to the view controller. An elegant solution for this requirement is to pass a *closure* into the location provider at initialization.

The Swift documentation defines closures as follows:

> Closures are self-contained blocks of functionality that can be passed around and used in your code.

They are often used to pass code that should be executed at some later time into a class or a struct. To learn more about closures, check out the Swift documentation.[2]

Open LocationProvider and add the following property right below the locationManager property:

---

2. https://docs.swift.org/swift-book/LanguageGuide/Closures.html

Map/Walk2Draw/Walk2Draw/Walk2Draw/LocationProvider.swift

```
private let updateHandler: (CLLocation) -> Void
```

Now that we have added a nonoptional property, we need to assign its value in the initializer. Replace the initializer with the following code. The changed line and the new line are highlighted.

Map/Walk2Draw/Walk2Draw/Walk2Draw/LocationProvider.swift

```
➤ init(updateHandler: @escaping (CLLocation) -> Void) {

    locationManager = CLLocationManager()
➤   self.updateHandler = updateHandler

    super.init()

    locationManager.delegate = self
    locationManager.distanceFilter = 1
    locationManager.requestWhenInUseAuthorization()
}
```

The only difference from what we did before is that we pass in an updateHandler and assign it to the updateHandler property. Note that we had to remove the override keyword because with the new parameter in the initializer we are not overriding any initializer of UIViewController anymore.

Whenever the locationManager registers a new location, we now have to call the updateHandler to pass the location to the view controller. Replace the body of locationManager(_:didUpdateLocations:) so that it looks like the following code:

Map/Walk2Draw/Walk2Draw/Walk2Draw/LocationProvider.swift

```
func locationManager(_ manager: CLLocationManager,
                     didUpdateLocations locations: [CLLocation]) {

  guard let location = locations.last else {
    return
  }
  updateHandler(location)
}
```

locationManager(_:didUpdateLocations:) provides the delegate with measured locations. From all the measured locations we need only one; that's why we call last on the locations array. Most of the time the locationManager will provide only one location. But if there's more than one location delivered in the array, the last one is the most accurate because the user might have moved in the meantime.

last is a calculated property defined on Array. Because an array can also be empty, last returns an optional. We need to unwrap it using a guard let statement before we can add it to the locations array.

If the locations array is empty, nothing needs to be done and we return. Otherwise, we call the updateHandler.

guard let

Here's how guard let works. If the value on the right side of the assignment in the guard let statement is nil, the code between the curly braces after the else is executed. Otherwise, the value is assigned to the nonoptional constant on the left side of the assignment and execution continues after the closing curly brace.

Go back to DrawViewController and add a property for the location provider.

Map/Walk2Draw/Walk2Draw/DrawViewController.swift

```swift
class DrawViewController: UIViewController {

  private var locationProvider: LocationProvider?

  override func loadView() {
    let contentView = DrawView(frame: .zero)

    view = contentView
  }
}
```

Before we move on with initializing this new property, let's import our LogStore library below the existing import statement.

Map/Walk2Draw/Walk2Draw/DrawViewController.swift

```swift
import UIKit
import LogStore
```

Next we need to initialize this property. A good place to do this is viewDidLoad():

Map/Walk2Draw/Walk2Draw/DrawViewController.swift

```swift
override func viewDidLoad() {
  super.viewDidLoad()

  locationProvider = LocationProvider(
    updateHandler: { location in

      printLog("location: \(location)")
  })
}
```

In this code we assign a new instance of LocationProvider to the new property and pass in an updateHandler that, for now, just prints the measured location.

To be able to start the location updates, we need an action for the Start button. Add the following method at the end of the DrawViewController class:

Map/Walk2Draw/Walk2Draw/DrawViewController.swift

```swift
@objc func startStop(_ sender: UIButton) {
  locationProvider?.start()
}
```

The @objc attribute is needed because otherwise the instance method is not exposed to the Objective-C runtime. Right now, under the hood, UIKit is written in Objective-C, but this might change in the future. Until then, we need to add @objc to methods used as actions in the target-action pattern.

You don't need to understand what this means exactly; just remember that this is how to connect buttons with actions in code. Don't worry, Xcode will remind you to add the @objc attribute when it's missing. You can learn more about attributes in the official Swift documentation.[3]

To hook up the Start button with this method, add the highlighted lines in the following code to loadView():

```
Map/Walk2Draw/Walk2Draw/DrawViewController.swift
override func loadView() {
  let contentView = DrawView(frame: .zero)
➤   contentView.startStopButton.addTarget(self,
➤                                 action: #selector(startStop(_:)),
➤                                 for: .touchUpInside)
  view = contentView
}
```

Whenever users release the touch while their finger is still within the bounds of the button, the action is executed.

Build and run the app on the simulator and click the Start button. Simulate different locations in the application menu Features > Location > Custom Location... of the simulator. As before, you should see location updates in the console of the debug area, but this time the locations are propagated to the view controller where we need them.

If you don't see the location updates in the log, make sure that you set up the location provider correctly and that you hooked up the target and the action of the startStopButton.

As its name suggests, the startStopButton acts as both the Start button and the Stop button. When the location updates are active, the button should have the title *Stop*, and when the user selects it, the location updates should stop. To keep track of the activity state of the location updates, we need a property. It's a good idea to add that state to the location provider because of the switch between the two states.

Open LocationProvider and add the following property below the updateHandler property:

---

3.   https://docs.swift.org/swift-book/ReferenceManual/Attributes.html

Map/Walk2Draw/Walk2Draw/LocationProvider.swift

```
private(set) var updating = false
```

With private(set), we tell the compiler that this property can be changed only from within the class it belongs to. From outside of this class, the property behaves like a constant. To update the value of this property when the location updates start, add the highlighted line in the following code at the end of the start() method:

Map/Walk2Draw/Walk2Draw/LocationProvider.swift

```
func start() {
  locationManager.startUpdatingLocation()
➤ updating = true
}
```

Next we need a method to stop the location updates. Add the following method to LocationProvider:

Map/Walk2Draw/Walk2Draw/LocationProvider.swift

```
func stop() {
  locationManager.stopUpdatingLocation()
  updating = false
}
```

This stop() method is the exact opposite of the start() method.

Switch back to the DrawViewController and replace the body of the startStop(_:) method with the highlighted lines in the following code:

Map/Walk2Draw/Walk2Draw/DrawViewController.swift

```
@objc func startStop(_ sender: UIButton) {
➤   guard let locationProvider = locationProvider else {
➤     fatalError()
➤   }
➤
➤   if locationProvider.updating {
➤     locationProvider.stop()
➤     sender.setTitle("Start", for: .normal)
➤   } else {
➤     locationProvider.start()
➤     sender.setTitle("Stop", for: .normal)
➤   }
}
```

First we unwrap the location provider using guard let because it is an Optional. It is possible—and common—to shadow the optional variable by using the same name for the unwrapped constant. The if condition checks if the locationProvider is updating right now, and we start or stop the location updates accordingly. In addition, we change the title on the Start/Stop button.

Build and run the app on the simulator and verify that you can start and stop location updates using the Start/Stop button.

Drawing on the Map

To be able to draw the path on the map, we need to store the locations arriving at the view controller somewhere. Because the locations are of type CLLocation, we have to import CoreLocation into DrawViewController.swift:

Map/Walk2Draw/Walk2Draw/DrawViewController.swift

```
import UIKit
import LogStore
import CoreLocation
```

Next, add the following property below the locationProvider property:

Map/Walk2Draw/Walk2Draw/DrawViewController.swift

```
private var locations: [CLLocation] = []
```

When the locationProvider passes a location via the update handler into the view controller, we add it to the array. Replace the initialization of the locationProvider with the highlighted lines in the following code:

Map/Walk2Draw/Walk2Draw/DrawViewController.swift

```
override func viewDidLoad() {
  super.viewDidLoad()

➤  locationProvider = LocationProvider(
➤    updateHandler: { [weak self] location in
➤
➤      guard let self = self else {
➤        return
➤      }
➤      printLog("location: \(location)")
➤      self.locations.append(location)
➤  })
}
```

With this code we add the location that gets passed into the update handler to the locations array property. self is *weakly captured* by the closure (see What Does [weak self] Do?, on page 22); this means within the closure self is an optional. We need to unwrap it with a guard let statement before we can use it.

Now, finally, comes the fun part: drawing on the map. MKMapViews can present additional data through map annotations and overlays. We're going to use a special overlay to add the path: MKPolyline.

Drawing is the responsibility of the view. Open DrawView and add the following method:

> \\//
> ~~
> **Joe asks:**
> # What Does [weak self] Do?
>
> When objects in a program are not used anymore, the memory they occupy should be made available for new objects. Swift manages this task for us using a concept called *Automatic Reference Counting (ARC)*. The compiler analyzes the code and figures out where memory can be freed again. As the name suggests, this happens automatically at compile time using reference counts.
>
> In some situations, we need to help the compiler figure out the ownership of objects. This is often the case when we use closures. Look at the code for the closure again. The closure calls self.locations.append(_:). self is the instance of DrawViewController in which this is called. By calling self.locations.append(_:), the closure "captures" self. This increases its reference count.
>
> This alone is not a problem. But in this case, the locationProvider owns the closure, and self owns the locationProvider. A construct like this is called a *reference cycle* because ownership is managed internally using references to objects. Because ARC counts only references, it won't free up memory when the instance of DrawViewController isn't used anymore.
>
> To break the cycle, we tell the compiler with [weak self] that the closure shouldn't increase the reference count of self. This way, the reference from the closure to self doesn't prevent self from being freed, and the cycle is broken.

Map/Walk2Draw/Walk2Draw/DrawView.swift

```swift
func addOverlay(with locations: [CLLocation]) {

  mapView.removeOverlays(mapView.overlays)

  let coordinates = locations.map { $0.coordinate }
  let overlay = MKPolyline(coordinates: coordinates,
                              count: coordinates.count)

  mapView.addOverlay(overlay)

  guard let lastCoordinate = coordinates.last else {
    return
  }

  let region = MKCoordinateRegion(center: lastCoordinate,
                                  latitudinalMeters: 300,
                                  longitudinalMeters: 300)
  mapView.setRegion(region, animated: true)
}
```

There's a lot going on in this code, so let's break it down. First we remove any overlay that might be on the map from the last call of this method. We need to do this because we can only draw the whole path at once. Next we map the locations array to an array of CLLocationCoordinate2Ds because this is what we need next. Then we create a polyline using these coordinates and add it as an overlay to the map.

The API for creating an instance of MKPolyline is a glimpse into the past. We need to pass in the array with the coordinates as well as the number of elements in the array. MKPolyline cannot figure out the number of the elements itself because under the hood the initializer gets only a pointer to the memory address of the array. To figure out the size of each element, it also needs the number of elements.

Finally we set the region of the map such that users can see what they're drawing.

We call this method from the updateHandler closure in viewDidLoad() of DrawViewController. Add the highlighted line in the following code at the end of the closure:

```
Map/Walk2Draw/Walk2Draw/DrawViewController.swift
override func viewDidLoad() {
  super.viewDidLoad()

  locationProvider = LocationProvider(
    updateHandler: { [weak self] location in

      guard let self = self else {
        return
      }
      printLog("location: \(location)")
      self.locations.append(location)

      (self.view as? DrawView)?.addOverlay(with: self.locations)
  })
}
```

Even though we assigned an instance of DrawView to the view property in load-View(), Xcode still sees the type UIView. Therefore, before accessing instance methods, we have to cast the view to the class DrawView.

This code is quite ugly and hard to read, so let's improve it before we move on. The reason this line of code is so ugly is the cast to DrawView. To remove the necessity for the cast, add the following calculated property below the existing stored properties:

```
Map/Walk2Draw/Walk2Draw/DrawViewController.swift
private var contentView: DrawView {
  view as! DrawView
}
```

This code downcasts the view of the view controller to DrawView. With this addition, we can change the call to addOverlay(with:) with this line:

Map/Walk2Draw/Walk2Draw/DrawViewController.swift

```
self.contentView.addOverlay(with: self.locations)
```

Build and run the app on the simulator and click the start button. Simulate different locations using the simulator menu. Oh...bummer, the path isn't shown on the map. The reason is that we didn't tell the map how to draw the path yet.

Go back to DrawView and add the highlighted line in the following code to the initializer, right below backgroundColor = UIColor.white:

Map/Walk2Draw/Walk2Draw/DrawView.swift

```
override init(frame: CGRect) {

  // ...
  // setup of the map and the buttons
  // ...

  super.init(frame: frame)

  backgroundColor = .white

➤ mapView.delegate = self

  // ...
  // setup stack views and activate constraints
  // ...
}
```

The mapView asks its delegate how it should draw the overlay. More precisely, it asks for a renderer to be used by the map view to render the path onto the map.

Next, add the following extension outside of DrawView but inside the file DrawView.swift:

Map/Walk2Draw/Walk2Draw/DrawView.swift

```
// MARK: - MKMapViewDelegate
extension DrawView : MKMapViewDelegate {
  func mapView(_ mapView: MKMapView,
               rendererFor overlay: MKOverlay)
    -> MKOverlayRenderer {

      if overlay is MKPolyline {
        let renderer = MKPolylineRenderer(overlay: overlay)
        renderer.strokeColor = .red
        renderer.lineWidth = 3
        return renderer
      } else {
        return MKOverlayRenderer(overlay: overlay)
      }
  }
}
```

The method mapView(_:rendererFor:) is called by the mapView on its delegate. If the overlay passed into this delegate method is the polyline we added earlier, we create an instance of MKPolylineRenderer and set it up to render the path.

Build and run the app on the simulator and start the location updates. Simulate different locations using the simulator menu and verify that you finally can draw on the map! Good work!

Connect your iPhone to your Mac and load the app onto your iPhone. Then go outside and experiment with the app. While using it, take notes in the Notes app about what's strange and what doesn't work. Then come back to make some final refinements.

Refining the Details

I hope you went out and tried the app. I did!

After using the app outside, this is what I noticed and what I'd like to improve:

1. The region the map shows is fixed to a square of 300 meters by 300 meters. It would be nice if the region adjusted to show the completely drawn path.

2. When the app is moved into the background, the location updates stop. The app should continue to record the path when running in the background.

3. The Clear button should clear the path.

4. The Share button should allow us to share the path.

Let's fix these problems one at a time.

Open DrawView and replace the code starting at the guard let statement in addOverlay(with:) with the highlighted lines in the following code:

Map/Walk2Draw/Walk2Draw/DrawView.swift

```
func addOverlay(with locations: [CLLocation]) {

  mapView.removeOverlays(mapView.overlays)

  let coordinates = locations.map { $0.coordinate }
  let overlay = MKPolyline(coordinates: coordinates,
                           count: coordinates.count)

  mapView.addOverlay(overlay)

➤ guard let lastLocation = locations.last else {
➤   return
➤ }
➤
➤ let maxDistance = locations.reduce(100) {
➤   result, next -> Double in
➤
➤   let distance = next.distance(from: lastLocation)
➤   return max(result, distance)
➤ }
➤
➤ let region = MKCoordinateRegion(
➤   center: lastLocation.coordinate,
➤   latitudinalMeters: maxDistance,
➤   longitudinalMeters: maxDistance)
➤
➤ mapView.setRegion(region, animated: true)
}
```

First we calculate the maximum distance of all the locations from the last location using reduce. reduce is a method defined on Sequence that allows us to process all the values of a sequence (for example, an array) down to a single value. We have to define a start value (100 in this case) and what we'd like to do with each value of the sequence. The code we've written takes each value of the locations array, calculates the distance to the last recorded location, and returns the maximum of that value and that of the previous step. The result of this reduce call is the maximum distance of all locations in the array to the last recorded location.

In this case, a start value of 100 means that the minimal maxDistance returned from the reduce call will be 100.

Build and run the app in the simulator, click the Start button, and simulate different locations in the simulator menu. The map zooms out when the path grows such that nearly the whole path is shown all the time.

To allow location updates in the background, we first need to add the required background mode to our app. Open the target settings and select the Signing & Capabilities tab. Click the + Capability button, as shown in the following image:

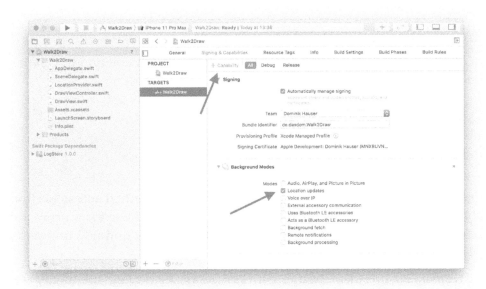

Add Background Modes with a double-click and select the "Location updates" check box. With this capability the app will be able to receive location updates when running in the background. To make the feature work, we need to activate it in the locationManager.

Open LocationProvider and add the highlighted line in the following code at the end of the start() method:

Map/Walk2Draw/Walk2Draw/LocationProvider.swift

```
func start() {
  locationManager.startUpdatingLocation()
  updating = true
  locationManager.allowsBackgroundLocationUpdates = true
}
```

It's good practice to disable location updates in the background when the stop button is tapped. Add the highlighted line at the end of the stop() method:

Map/Walk2Draw/Walk2Draw/LocationProvider.swift

```
func stop() {
  locationManager.stopUpdatingLocation()
  updating = false
  locationManager.allowsBackgroundLocationUpdates = false
}
```

You might be wondering why our app can access the device location when it is not in the foreground. We asked for permission to access the user's location when the app is in use. When our app is running in the background, it is still in use, and users can tell that it is accessing their location by the blue indicator in the status bar.

Implementing the Clear and Share Buttons

To implement the Clear button, add this method for the action to DrawViewController:

```
Map/Walk2Draw/Walk2Draw/DrawViewController.swift
@objc func clear(_ sender: UIButton) {
  locations.removeAll()

  contentView.addOverlay(with: locations)
}
```

Again, we need to add the @objc attribute to make this method accessible from Objective-C. This method removes all locations from the locations array and then calls addOverlay(with:) to remove the existing overlay and add an overlay with an empty path.

Next, hook up the Clear button with the action by adding the highlighted lines in the following code to loadView(), right below the code that adds the target and action to the startStopButton:

```
Map/Walk2Draw/Walk2Draw/DrawViewController.swift
override func loadView() {
  let contentView = DrawView(frame: .zero)

  contentView.startStopButton.addTarget(self,
                              action: #selector(startStop(_:)),
                              for: .touchUpInside)

➤  contentView.clearButton.addTarget(self,
➤                            action: #selector(clear(_:)),
➤                            for: .touchUpInside)
  view = contentView
}
```

Build and run the app, and verify that the Clear button works.

Sharing is caring, and your friends and followers want to see your creations, so our little app needs the ability to share the drawn image to social media. MapKit has a class called MKMapSnapshotter that allows us to create an image from a given map region. Import MapKit below the existing import statements:

Map/Walk2Draw/Walk2Draw/DrawViewController.swift

```swift
import UIKit
import LogStore
import CoreLocation
import MapKit
```

Then add the following method:

Map/Walk2Draw/Walk2Draw/DrawViewController.swift

```swift
@objc func share(_ sender: UIButton) {

  if locations.isEmpty {
    return
  }

  let options = MKMapSnapshotter.Options()
  options.region = contentView.mapView.region

  let snapshotter = MKMapSnapshotter(options: options)
  snapshotter.start { snapshot, error in
  }
}
```

If there are no locations recorded, we return from this method and do nothing. Otherwise, this method sets the map region in an instance of MKMapSnapshotter.Options, creates an instance of MKMapSnapshotter with these options, and calls start(completionHandler:) on that instance. The snapshotter creates the snapshot of the region and calls the completion handler with the result when it's finished.

We can now add a target and an action for the share method to the Share button in loadView():

Map/Walk2Draw/Walk2Draw/DrawViewController.swift

```swift
override func loadView() {
  let contentView = DrawView(frame: .zero)

  contentView.startStopButton.addTarget(self,
                                action: #selector(startStop(_:)),
                                for: .touchUpInside)

  contentView.clearButton.addTarget(self,
                                action: #selector(clear(_:)),
                                for: .touchUpInside)

➤ contentView.shareButton.addTarget(self,
➤                               action: #selector(share(_:)),
➤                               for: .touchUpInside)

  view = contentView
}
```

When setting up the snapshotter, we can provide only the map region the snapshot should show. To add the path to the snapshot, we need to add the following helper method to DrawViewController:

```
Map/Walk2Draw/Walk2Draw/DrawViewController.swift
func imageByAddingPath(
  with locations: [CLLocation],
  to snapshot: MKMapSnapshotter.Snapshot)
  -> UIImage {

    UIGraphicsBeginImageContextWithOptions(
      snapshot.image.size, true, snapshot.image.scale)

    snapshot.image.draw(at: .zero)

    let bezierPath = UIBezierPath()
    guard let firstCoordinate = locations.first?.coordinate else {
      fatalError("locations array is empty")
    }
    let firstPoint = snapshot.point(for: firstCoordinate)
    bezierPath.move(to: firstPoint)

    for location in locations.dropFirst() {
      let point = snapshot.point(for: location.coordinate)
      bezierPath.addLine(to: point)
    }

    UIColor.red.setStroke()
    bezierPath.lineWidth = 2
    bezierPath.stroke()

    guard let image = UIGraphicsGetImageFromCurrentImageContext() else {
      fatalError("could not get image from context")
    }
    UIGraphicsEndImageContext()

    return image
}
```

This code creates an image context and draws the image from the snapshot into it. Then it creates a *Bézier path* from the locations and draws that into the context as well. A Bézier path is just a path that can be drawn on a view. We set the start point with the call bezierPath.move(to: firstPoint). Then we iterate over the rest of the locations and add lines between the points with the call bezier-Path.addLine(to: point). To transform the map coordinates to view coordinates for the Bézier path, we use the method point(for:) defined in MKMapSnapshotter.Snapshot.

Finally, we set the stroke color and the line width and tell the bezierPath to draw itself by calling stroke(). We get the resulting image from the current image context and return it to the caller.

This is how you create an image in iOS. It looks a bit strange because of the image context we have to set up and draw into, but this is how it's done.

Now we can use this helper method in the completion handler of the start(completionHandler:) method of the snapshotter:

Map/Walk2Draw/Walk2Draw/DrawViewController.swift

```swift
@objc func share(_ sender: UIButton) {

  if locations.isEmpty {
    return
  }

  let options = MKMapSnapshotter.Options()
  options.region = contentView.mapView.region

  let snapshotter = MKMapSnapshotter(options: options)
  snapshotter.start { snapshot, error in
    guard let snapshot = snapshot else {
      return
    }
    let image = self.imageByAddingPath(
      with: self.locations,
      to: snapshot)

    let activity = UIActivityViewController(
      activityItems: [image, "#walk2draw"],
      applicationActivities: nil)
    self.present(activity, animated: true)
  }
}
```

Note that at the end of the closure we create an instance of UIActivityViewController with this image and present it to the user. The UIActivityViewController is the standard share sheet in iOS that lets users share many different types of content (images, text, contact information, and so on) with apps that support those types. In our example, the share sheet presents apps, such as Twitter and Facebook, that can work with images.

The share sheet also includes a button to save the image in the photos library. To make this work, we need to add a usage description for the key NSPhotoLibraryAddUsageDescription to the Info.plist. Open Info.plist, create a new entry by clicking the plus sign in one of the existing entries, and type in the key NSPhotoLibraryAddUsageDescription. Add the following description for the value: "An image of a map with your walking path is added to your library."

Build and run the app, record a path, and touch the Share button. It works! The app is finished. With this app the user can draw paths on maps, like the image you see on page 32, and share the result with friends and family.

Exercises

1. Add error handling to the code. For example, you could present an alert to the users if they haven't authorized the use of the device location.

2. Change the code so the user can "lift" the "pencil" and continue the drawing at another place.

    Hint: Use an array of arrays of CLLocations.

3. Add a label to the user interface that shows the walked distance.

    Hint: Change the reduce call in addOverlay(with:) to a for loop and sum the distances between consecutive locations.

4. Make the paths conform to Codable and implement storing and retrieving of previous paths.

    Hint: Search the Internet for Codable. There are many examples online.

Everything every day here on Earth is based on gravity, and you
don't realize it until you don't have it anymore.

➤ *Peggy Whitson*

CHAPTER 2

Measuring Length with Gravitation

When it comes to physics phenomena, sometimes our intuition about what's going on does not reflect reality. For example, two bodies with different masses experience the same acceleration when falling down in the gravitational field of the Earth. You might remember the experiment from school or from an online video where a feather and a rock fall in a vacuum. Without any surrounding air to create friction, they take the same time to hit the ground.

The same is true for swinging on a swing at the playground. No matter how heavy someone is, the period of the swing is always the same. It depends only on the length of the swing and the gravitational acceleration.

In this chapter we'll use the iPhone's built-in accelerometer to measure the period of a swing. With this value we'll be able to calculate the length of the swing and display it in the user interface. In addition we will use the Core Graphics framework to draw the collected data on-screen. The user interface will be built using a storyboard and the Interface Builder in Xcode.

The result will look like a sophisticated measuring device as shown in the image on page 34, even though the code we need to achieve this isn't complicated.

After working through this chapter, you'll be able read the sensor data from an iPhone and present many kinds of data to your users.

You can use the sensor data in your own apps, for example, to add some playfulness to your user interface. This might prompt people to load your apps just because they're fun to play with. The Core Graphics framework can do more than just draw data points onto the screen. By dipping your toe into Core Graphics, you'll be taking the first step toward drawing custom user interfaces. This also can make your apps stand out from the millions of others in the App Store.

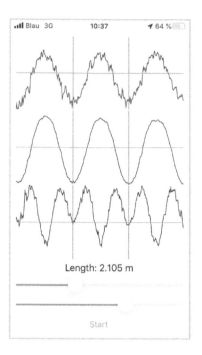

Setting Up the Project

Open Xcode and create a new Single View App using the shortcut ⇧⌘N. For Product Name type in MeasureSwing, select Storyboard for the User Interface, and click Next. In the next window, select a location on your Mac for the project and click Create.

Next let's add our logging library to the project. Select the menu item File > Swift Packages > Add Package Dependency, type https://github.com/dasdom/LogStore2.git into the search field, and press return. Click Next and then Finish. To activate the logging library, add the highlighted lines in the following code to SceneDelegate:

Sensors/MeasureSwing/MeasureSwing/SceneDelegate.swift

```
import UIKit
➤ import LogStore

class SceneDelegate: UIResponder, UIWindowSceneDelegate {

  var window: UIWindow?
➤  var trigger: LogTrigger?

  func scene(_ scene: UIScene,
             willConnectTo session: UISceneSession,
             options connectionOptions: UIScene.ConnectionOptions) {

    guard let _ = (scene as? UIWindowScene) else { return }
```

```
➤     #if DEBUG
➤     trigger = LogTrigger(in: window)
➤     #endif
    }

    // ...
    // other methods
    // ...
}
```

Collecting Motion Data

Apps register for data from the acceleration sensors through an instance of
CMMotionManger defined in the framework CoreMotion. Open ViewController.swift and
import CoreMotion right below the existing import statement. Then import the
LogStore logging library:

Sensors/MeasureSwing/MeasureSwing/ViewController.swift
```
import UIKit
import CoreMotion
import LogStore
```

We need a property for the CMMotionManager instance. Add the highlighted
property declaration in the following code at the beginning of ViewController:

Sensors/MeasureSwing/MeasureSwing/ViewController.swift
```
class ViewController: UIViewController {

➤   let motionManager = CMMotionManager()

    override func viewDidLoad() {
      super.viewDidLoad()
      // Do any additional setup after loading the view.

    }
}
```

Next, add the following method to ViewController:

Sensors/MeasureSwing/MeasureSwing/ViewController.swift
```
func startMotionUpdates() {

  motionManager.deviceMotionUpdateInterval = 1 / 60

  motionManager.startDeviceMotionUpdates(
    using: .xArbitraryZVertical,
    to: OperationQueue()) { motion, error in

      guard let motion = motion else {
        return
      }
      printLog("motion: \(motion)")
  }
}
```

In the first line of this method, we set the update interval for the motion events. This tells the motion manager that we'd like to have at most sixty events per second. The actual update interval depends on the capabilities of the iPhone hardware.

Then we have to start the motion updates using the method startDeviceMotionUpdates(using:to:withHandler:) on motionManager. The first parameter tells the motion manager the reference frame it should use for the attitude samples. .xArbitraryZVertical means that the z-axis is vertical and the x-axis points to an arbitrary direction in the horizontal plane, as shown in the following image:

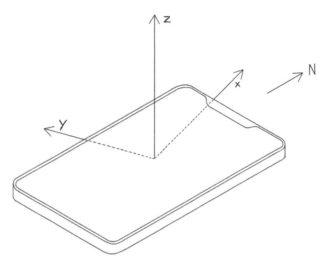

Using an arbitrary direction for the x-axis means the iPhone doesn't need to calibrate the magnetometer beforehand. As we are interested only in relative movements of the iPhone, we don't care where north is.

The second parameter is the operation queue UIKit should use to process the data. The documentation states that it's not recommended to use the main operation queue because the processed events might arrive at a higher rate. That's why we create a new operation queue with the default configuration for this parameter.

The last parameter is a closure the motion manager calls on the given operation queue when motion updates are available. Because we've set the deviceMotionUpdateInterval to 1 / 60, we expect that this closure is called about sixty times per second. This means we should optimize the computation done in that closure for performance. The closure is called with two parameters, an optional CMDeviceMotion and an optional Error. In this example, we just unwrap and print the motion that contains all of the device's motion information.

To see the motion events in action, add the highlighted line in the following code at the end of viewDidLoad() and build and run the app on your iPhone:

```
Sensors/MeasureSwing/MeasureSwing/ViewController.swift
override func viewDidLoad() {
  super.viewDidLoad()
  // Do any additional setup after loading the view.

  startMotionUpdates()
}
```

Activate the console with the keyboard shortcut ⇧⌘C. On the bottom right, you should see the motion events pouring in as shown in the following image:

Nice! We're able to read motion data with just a few lines of code.

If you don't see any motion events in the console, make sure you call startMotionUpdates() in viewDidLoad().

Before we move on, let's rename the class ViewController to a more fitting name. Double-click the class name in the class declaration line and select the menu item Editor > Refactor > Rename. Wait until Xcode finishes scanning the project for the usage of that name. Change the name to MeasurementViewController. Xcode should look something like the image on page 38.

To initiate the renaming, click the Rename button at the upper left.

Pro Tip: If Renaming Fails

Sometimes renaming this way doesn't work. In this case, Xcode shows the file name in red in the project navigator. To fix this problem, navigate to the location of the file in the file system and rename it manually. Now Xcode shows the file name in black again.

Storing Acceleration Data

We need to store the collected data to be able to draw it in the next step. The accelerometer of the iPhone collects data for each axis of the device—we get three Double values in each event. As the update interval of the events depends on the current state of the hardware, we also need to store the event's timestamp so that later we'll be able to calculate the swing's frequency. Add a new Swift file using the shortcut ⌘N. Save the file as AccelerationData.swift.

Add the following struct to the file:

Sensors/MeasureSwing/MeasureSwing/AccelerationData.swift
```
struct AccelerationData {
  let timestamp: TimeInterval
  let value: Double
}
```

The struct has two properties, one for storing the timestamp of the event and one for storing the actual value. The type TimeInterval is defined in Foundation, and it is just a typealias for Double. Type aliases are often used to make code more readable. This way the type of timestamp gives us additional information about the usage of that property.

Pro Tip: typealias for Your Own Types

You can define your own type aliases. For example, when you have a property for a duration of seconds, you could define a type alias with typealias Second = Float. Then you can use Second interchangeably with Float. If requirements change later in the development process and Second needs to become an Int, you only have to change the type once.

Note that we don't have to add an initializer because AccelerationData is a structure and, as such, gets a default initializer. It's a good idea to use a struct here because the acceleration data is best represented by value type. To learn more about the difference between classes and structures, and when to use which, see the Swift documentation.[1]

Now we can add an array to store the motion events. Open the class MeasurementViewController and add the highlighted property below the motionManager property:

Sensors/MeasureSwing/MeasureSwing/MeasurementViewController.swift

```
let motionManager = CMMotionManager()
➤ var xAccelerationData: [AccelerationData] = []
```

For now we need only one array for the x-axis—later we'll add arrays for the other axes too.

To fill the array with acceleration data, add the highlighted lines in the following code to the method startMotionUpdates():

Sensors/MeasureSwing/MeasureSwing/MeasurementViewController.swift

```
func startMotionUpdates() {

    motionManager.deviceMotionUpdateInterval = 1 / 60

    motionManager.startDeviceMotionUpdates(
      using: .xArbitraryZVertical,
      to: OperationQueue()) { motion, error in

        guard let motion = motion else {
          return
        }

➤       let acceleration = motion.userAcceleration
➤       let timestamp = motion.timestamp
➤       let xData = AccelerationData(timestamp: timestamp,
➤                                   value: acceleration.x)
➤
➤       DispatchQueue.main.async {
➤         self.xAccelerationData.append(xData)
➤       }
    }
}
```

With guard let, we unwrap the optional motion value. This means the program continues after the closing curly brace only if motion is not nil. In this case, the value is assigned to the nonoptional constant motion on the left side of the equal sign.

---

1. https://docs.swift.org/swift-book/LanguageGuide/ClassesAndStructures.html

Even if the device is lying flat on the table, the accelerometer measures an acceleration—the gravitation. (The equivalence of acceleration and gravitation was first formulated by Albert Einstein in his general theory of relativity.) Fortunately, Apple provides us with a value where the gravitation is already deducted: userAcceleration. We assign this value to a constant because it makes the code that follows easier to read.

Next, we create an instance of AccelerationData with the timestamp of the motion event and the x-value of the acceleration. This instance is then added to the array of acceleration data for the x-axis.

Note that we have removed the print() method because we don't need it anymore.

Now that we have the data, we need a user interface to show it. We're going to use a storyboard for the user interface.

Building the User Interface Using a Storyboard

Open Main.storyboard by clicking it in the project navigator in Xcode. Open the library with the keyboard shortcut ⇧⌘L and drag a Vertical Stack View onto the Measurement View Controller Scene. Select the stack view and click the Add New Constraints button—the one with a square between two vertical lines—in the lower right of the Xcode editor view. Pin the stack view to the safe area of the super view by entering a value of 10 in the four text fields in the upper third of the constraints pop-up. Click the red constraint markers next to the text fields if they are not active and select the "Constrain to margins" check box. The relevant part of the user interface in the Interface Builder should look like the following image:

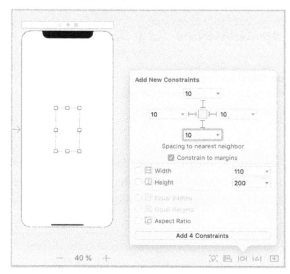

Click the button Add 4 Constraints. With these constraints, we pin the stack view to the safe area of the scenes view. Xcode updates the frame of the stack view according to the new constraints. But because the stack view has no background color, its frame is visible only when it is selected.

The Interface Builder has a setting that helps in such situations. You can activate a thin blue border around all the elements in a storyboard scene through the Xcode menu item Editor > Canvas > Bounds Rectangles. This border helps a lot while you're setting up the user interface. Don't worry; it is visible only in the Interface Builder and not in the running app.

Pro Tip: Distances in Interface Builder

If you hold down the option key and hover over elements in a scene, the Interface Builder shows you the distance from the selected element to all its neighbors. This is useful if you need to make the app look like a design given to you by the designer.

Next we need a view that will draw the acceleration data. Open the library again with ⇧⌘L, search for UIView, and drag a view onto the stack view. The following image shows how this should look. Note the view hierarchy in the structure overview on the left side of the storyboard.

Then open the library with the shortcut ⇧⌘L again and drag a button onto the stack view below the previously added view. Make sure that you drop it into, not below, the stack view. If you drop it at the wrong spot, delete it and try again. With the button selected, open the attributes inspector using the shortcut ⌥⌘5 and change the button title to Start. This button will start and stop the recording of motion events.

The scene now has a vertical stack view with a view and a button. This is enough user interface work for the moment, but we'll add more elements later in this chapter.

Next, we connect the Start/Stop button with the view controller. The easiest way to do this is to click the button with the five lines in the upper-right corner of the Interface Builder. Xcode opens a menu where you can select Assistant. Alternatively, you can use the shortcut ⌃⌥⌘↩.

Pro Tip: Shortcuts

Whenever you realize that you do the same task in Xcode over and over again, try to figure out if there is a shortcut for it. You can see many of the available Xcode shortcuts in the Xcode application menus. Once you have learned the shortcuts for the tasks you do every day, you work way faster than when you're relying solely on a mouse or trackpad.

Xcode opens the file with the code for the currently selected storyboard scene side by side with the storyboard. Press and hold the `control` key and drag a connection from the button in the storyboard to the view controller right above the closing curly braces. It should look like the following image:

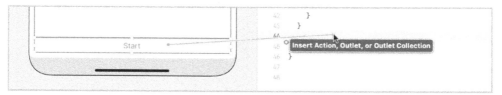

Xcode presents a pop-up for the options of the action we're going to add. In the Name text field, type startStop and select UIButton in the Type drop-down menu. Whenever you create an action by dragging from an element in a storyboard scene, set the type in the action to the type of the element. If you don't change the type, Xcode will use the type Any for the sender, and valuable information will be lost. Make sure the connection is set to Action (not Outlet) and then click Connect.

Add the highlighted line to the generated startStop(_:) method:

```
Sensors/MeasureSwing/MeasureSwing/MeasurementViewController.swift
@IBAction func startStop(_ sender: UIButton) {
    startMotionUpdates()
}
```

Instead of starting the collection of motion data in viewDidLoad(), we'll start it when the user taps the Start button. Now delete the whole viewDidLoad() method; we won't need it anymore.

In the next section, we'll build a view that draws the collected data on-screen.

Drawing Data

Create a new file with the shortcut ⌘N and choose the Cocoa Touch Class template. In the Class text field, type in the name DiagramView and make it a subclass of UIView. Click Next and then click Create.

Xcode creates a subclass of UIView and fills it with some comments to get us started. Remove the lines with the comments and the multiline comment strings such that the class looks like this:

Sensors/MeasureSwing/MeasureSwing/DiagramView.swift
```
class DiagramView: UIView {
  override func draw(_ rect: CGRect) {
  }
}
```

UIKit calls the draw method of a UIView subclass whenever the view is rendered on-screen. We have to put our drawing code into this method. But before we can draw data, we need to have it available in the view class. Add the following property to DiagramView:

Sensors/MeasureSwing/MeasureSwing/DiagramView.swift
```
class DiagramView: UIView {

➤   var dataArray: [AccelerationData] = []

    override func draw(_ rect: CGRect) {
    }
}
```

Next, add the highlighted code to the draw(_:) method:

Sensors/MeasureSwing/MeasureSwing/DiagramView.swift
```
override func draw(_ rect: CGRect) {

➤   let width = frame.size.width
➤   let height = frame.size.height
➤   let y0 = height/2.0
➤
➤   var maximum = 0.0
➤   for data in dataArray {
➤     maximum = max(maximum, abs(data.value))
➤   }
}
```

The view doesn't know about acceleration or time frames, but it knows the frame it needs to draw. To be able to scale the acceleration data and the time values to the available space in the view, we assign the width and the height of the view and the maximum of all values to constants. In addition, we store half the height to use it later as the vertical zero line.

The data will be drawn using an instance of UIBezierPath, which is a path consisting of line segments that we can render in our custom views. Add the highlighted code to draw(_:):

Sensors/MeasureSwing/MeasureSwing/DiagramView.swift

```
override func draw(_ rect: CGRect) {

  let width = frame.size.width
  let height = frame.size.height
  let y0 = height/2.0

  var maximum = 0.0
  for data in dataArray {
    maximum = max(maximum, abs(data.value))
  }
➤  let bezierPath = UIBezierPath()
➤
➤  guard let firstPoint = dataArray.first,
➤    let lastPoint = dataArray.last,
➤    maximum > 0 else {
➤      return
➤  }
➤  let scale = height / (CGFloat(maximum) * 2.0)
➤  let y = y0 + CGFloat(firstPoint.value) * scale
➤  bezierPath.move(to: CGPoint(x: 0, y: y))
  }
```

The properties first and last defined on Array return the first and the last element, respectively. If the array is empty, these values are nil; if the array has only one element, first and last both return this element. To scale the values in the diagram for optimal presentation, we'll divide by maximum. Dividing by zero is mathematically not allowed, so we need to make sure that we proceed only when maximum is greater than zero.

Next we calculate the scale for the acceleration values. Because the zero line is a horizontal line through the center of the view, we have to scale the values to half the height of the view. Then we calculate the first value using the zero value y0 and the scaled value of the data point. We add this value to the Bézier path using the move(to:) method. Think about this like drawing with a pencil. Before we draw the first segment, we have to move the pencil to the location where the segment should start.

Now add the highlighted lines to the end of draw(_:):

Sensors/MeasureSwing/MeasureSwing/DiagramView.swift

```
override func draw(_ rect: CGRect) {

  // ...
  // define constraints
  // ...

  let bezierPath = UIBezierPath()

  guard let firstPoint = dataArray.first,
    let lastPoint = dataArray.last,
    maximum > 0 else {
      return
  }
  let scale = height / (CGFloat(maximum) * 2.0)
  let y = y0 + CGFloat(firstPoint.value) * scale
  bezierPath.move(to: CGPoint(x: 0, y: y))
➤ let totalTime = lastPoint.timestamp - firstPoint.timestamp
➤ if totalTime == 0 {
➤   return
➤ }
➤ for dataPoint in dataArray {
➤   let timeDiff = dataPoint.timestamp - firstPoint.timestamp
➤   let x = CGFloat(timeDiff / totalTime) * width
➤   let y = y0 + CGFloat(dataPoint.value) * scale
➤   bezierPath.addLine(to: CGPoint(x: x, y: y))
➤ }
}
```

In this code we first calculate the total time frame of the collected data. This value will be used to scale the time values on the x-axis such that they span the whole width of the view. Because we're going to divide by the total time, we need to make sure that the value is not zero.

Then, for each data point, we calculate the x- and y-values for the corresponding point in the Bézier path. The x-value is the time difference to the first data point scaled to the width of the view using the total time frame. We calculate the y-value as we did for the first point. The result is added to the Bézier path using the addLine(to:) method.

The Bézier path is now complete and we can draw it with the highlighted lines in the following code:

Sensors/MeasureSwing/MeasureSwing/DiagramView.swift

```
override func draw(_ rect: CGRect) {

  // ...
  // define constraints
  // ...
```

```
// ...
// setup bezier path
// ...
```
➤ `UIColor.label.setStroke()`
➤ `bezierPath.lineWidth = 1`
➤ `bezierPath.stroke()`
```
}
```

The code sets the stroke color and the line width for the Bézier path and then draws it by calling stroke(). The color label should be used for static text and related elements. We use it here because this way the drawn line is visible in dark and light mode.

Now we can use the diagram view in the storyboard. Open Main.storyboard, select the blank view in the stack view, and open the identity inspector with the shortcut ⌥⌘4. Type DiagramView into the Class text field and hit return.

To update the diagram view when new acceleration data is available, first we need a reference to it in the view controller. If it's not already open, open the assistant editor using the shortcut ⌃⌥⌘↩. Press and hold control and drag a connection from the view into the code below the xAccelerationData property:

Make sure the connection is set to Outlet, type in the name xDiagramView, and click Connect.

Xcode adds the highlighted property to MeasurementViewController:

```
Sensors/MeasureSwing/MeasureSwing/MeasurementViewController.swift
let motionManager = CMMotionManager()
var xAccelerationData: [AccelerationData] = []
@IBOutlet var xDiagramView: DiagramView!
```

Next, replace the declaration of xAccelerationData with the following code:

```
Sensors/MeasureSwing/MeasureSwing/MeasurementViewController.swift
var xAccelerationData: [AccelerationData] = [] {
  didSet {
    xDiagramView.dataArray = xAccelerationData
  }
}
```

With this code we add a didSet observer to the xAccelerationData property. The didSet observer of a property is called immediately after a new value is assigned. In the observer, we pass the collected acceleration data to the diagram view.

Now we need to trigger the drawing of the data in the diagram view when new data arrives. Open DiagramView and replace the declaration of the dataArray property with the following code:

```
Sensors/MeasureSwing/MeasureSwing/DiagramView.swift
var dataArray: [AccelerationData] = [] {
  didSet {
    setNeedsDisplay()
  }
}
```

We use a didSet observer to tell the view that it should draw itself by calling setNeedsDisplay(). This triggers a call of the draw(_:) method.

Build and run the application on your iPhone, tap the Start button, and shake your device. The result should look something like the image on page 48.

How cool is that? With these few lines of code, we managed to read sensor data from the device and draw it on the view. I'm sure you have lots of ideas for what you can do with these new skills. But before you explore those ideas, let's finish our fun little app.

Starting and Stopping Motion Events

The user needs to be able to stop and restart collecting motion events. Add the following method to MeasurementViewController:

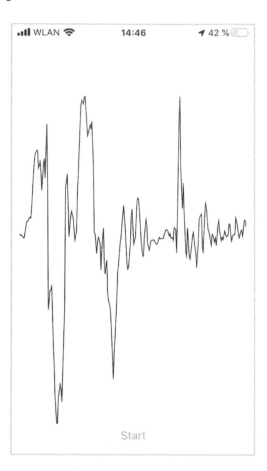

Sensors/MeasureSwing/MeasureSwing/MeasurementViewController.swift

```
func stopMotionUpdates() {
  motionManager.stopDeviceMotionUpdates()
}
```

This method stops the motion events by calling stopDeviceMotionUpdates() of our motionManager. Next, replace the body of the startStop(_:) method with the highlighted lines in the following code:

Sensors/MeasureSwing/MeasureSwing/MeasurementViewController.swift

```
@IBAction func startStop(_ sender: UIButton) {
  if motionManager.isDeviceMotionActive {
    sender.setTitle("Start", for: .normal)
    stopMotionUpdates()
  } else {
    sender.setTitle("Stop", for: .normal)
    startMotionUpdates()
  }
}
```

If the motionManager is collecting data at the moment, the value isDeviceMotionActive is true. In this case we set the title of the Start/Stop button to Start, and we call a method that stops the motion events. If the device motion is not active, we set the title of the button to Stop and start the motion events.

When restarting the collection of motion events, we should delete the old data. Add the highlighted line right before the call startDeviceMotionUpdates(using:to:with-Handler:) in startMotionUpdates():

Sensors/MeasureSwing/MeasureSwing/MeasurementViewController.swift
```
func startMotionUpdates() {

  motionManager.deviceMotionUpdateInterval = 1 / 60

➤  xAccelerationData = []

  motionManager.startDeviceMotionUpdates(
    using: .xArbitraryZVertical,
    to: OperationQueue()) { motion, error in

      guard let motion = motion else {
        return
      }
      let acceleration = motion.userAcceleration
      let timestamp = motion.timestamp
      let xData = AccelerationData(timestamp: timestamp,
                                   value: acceleration.x)

      DispatchQueue.main.async {
        self.xAccelerationData.append(xData)
      }
  }
}
```

With this line we remove all collected motion events from the array. Build and run the app on your iPhone and check if you can now start and stop motion events.

Three Axes of Motion

To measure the length of the swing, the user needs to measure the period of the swing by holding the phone while swinging. Depending on how the user holds the phone, showing only the data for one direction might not be enough to figure out the peaks of the motion. The iPhone can measure acceleration along three perpendicular axes (see the image showing the arbitrary x-axis on page 36). To make it easier to measure the length of the swing, we want to display all the acceleration data to the user.

Open Main.storyboard. If the assistant editor is still open, make sure the storyboard is selected by clicking somewhere in it. Use the shortcut ⇧⌘L to open the library, search for UIView, and drag a view between the existing diagram view and the Start button. Open the library again and drag another view below the diagram view. When you are finished with this, the structure of the measurement user interface should look like the following image:

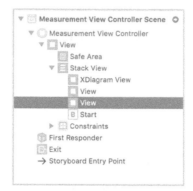

You might have noticed that there's a red circle with an arrow at the top of the structure overview as well as red lines in the scene of the measurement view controller. The Interface Builder uses these markers to tell us that something is wrong with the layout constraints. Layout constraints are responsible for defining the position and the size of each view in the user interface. You should always fix constraint errors even if the user interface seems to work; otherwise, it could break on some devices or for some users.

The problem right now in the user interface is that there are no constraints that define the height of each of the views in the stack view. To solve the problem, we could simply add those constraints, but there's an easier solution.

Select the diagram view and the two views we've just added by clicking each of them while holding down the `command` key. Then select the Xcode menu item Editor > Embed In > Stack View. Xcode adds a new vertical stack view and puts the selected views into it, but this doesn't solve the layout problem yet.

Select the new stack view and open the attribute inspector with the keyboard shortcut ⌥⌘5. In the attribute inspector, select Fill Equally from the Distribution drop-down list. This solves the layout problem because it tells the stack view that the containing views should all be of the same height. As we are already here, type the value 2 into the Spacing text field to improve the layout of the stack view. This adds a space of 2 points between the arranged subviews of the stack view.

Because the stack view will show the diagrams, its arranged views need to be instances of DiagramView. Select the two plain views while holding down the `command` key and open the identity inspector with ⌥⌘4. In the Class text field, type the name `DiagramView` and hit `return`. The result should look like the following image:

Your button might be much taller than the one in this image. The reason is that we haven't set the button's *hugging priority*. This means the button could have many different heights and the constraints would still be valid. A high hugging priority tells the button that it should try to make its size such that all content remains visible but no larger than that. It's like the button is pulling its edges inward.

Select the button and use the shortcut ⌥⌘6 to open the size inspector and set the vertical value in the section Content Hugging Priority to 750. It should look like the following image:

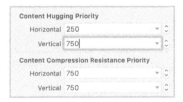

The view controller needs to hold references to the views to be able to fill them with the acceleration data. Open the assistant editor with ⌃⌥⌘↩ if it's not already open. Press and hold control and drag a connection from the first of the new views into the code below the existing xDiagramView property. Type in the name yDiagramView, make sure Connection is set to Outlet, and click Connect. Repeat these steps for the last diagram view and name the property zDiagramView.

Now that we have the diagram views for the y and z acceleration data, let's use them to draw the data. Open MeasurementViewController.swift and look for all the occurrences of xAccelerationData and xDiagramView. Let's add the corresponding statements for the y- and z-axes.

We'll start with the properties. Add the highlighted lines of the two properties right below the xAccelerationData property:

Sensors/MeasureSwing/MeasureSwing/MeasurementViewController.swift

```
class MeasurementViewController: UIViewController {

  let motionManager = CMMotionManager()
  var xAccelerationData: [AccelerationData] = [] {
    didSet {
      xDiagramView.dataArray = xAccelerationData
    }
  }
➤ var yAccelerationData: [AccelerationData] = [] {
➤   didSet {
➤     yDiagramView.dataArray = yAccelerationData
➤   }
➤ }
➤ var zAccelerationData: [AccelerationData] = [] {
➤   didSet {
➤     zDiagramView.dataArray = zAccelerationData
➤   }
➤ }

  @IBOutlet var xDiagramView: DiagramView!
  @IBOutlet var yDiagramView: DiagramView!
  @IBOutlet var zDiagramView: DiagramView!

  // ...
  // methods
  // ...
}
```

This is exactly the code we wrote before for the x data. Next, scroll to the method startMotionUpdates() and add the highlighted lines in the following code:

Sensors/MeasureSwing/MeasureSwing/MeasurementViewController.swift

```swift
func startMotionUpdates() {

  motionManager.deviceMotionUpdateInterval = 1 / 60

  xAccelerationData = []
➤ yAccelerationData = []
➤ zAccelerationData = []

  motionManager.startDeviceMotionUpdates(
    using: .xArbitraryZVertical,
    to: OperationQueue()) { motion, error in

      guard let motion = motion else {
        return
      }
      print("motion: \(motion)")

      let acceleration = motion.userAcceleration
      let timestamp = motion.timestamp
      let xData = AccelerationData(timestamp: timestamp,
                                     value: acceleration.x)
➤     let yData = AccelerationData(timestamp: timestamp,
➤                                    value: acceleration.y)
➤     let zData = AccelerationData(timestamp: timestamp,
➤                                    value: acceleration.z)

      DispatchQueue.main.async {
        self.xAccelerationData.append(xData)
➤       self.yAccelerationData.append(yData)
➤       self.zAccelerationData.append(zData)
      }
  }
}
```

This code is again exactly the same as for the x-axis. Build and run the app on your iPhone, and then start the collection of data and shake your device. If one of the diagram views doesn't show a data curve, make sure that the names are correct. It's easy to make copy-paste errors with this code.

To figure out the period of the motion, we need to measure the distance of two adjacent maximums or minimums in one of the diagrams. The easiest way to do this is to add movable markers to the diagrams. The user would then move the markers to the maximums.

Adding Movable Markers to the Diagrams

For the marker we need a user interface element that allows for the easy input of a value between 0 and 1. UIKit provides the class UISlider, which perfectly fits this task. Open Main.storyboard and use the shortcut ⇧⌘L to open the library. Search for Slider and drag one above the button at the same horizontal level as the button. If the slider is located in the diagram stack view or the lower diagram view, delete it and try again. Drag another slider between the existing slider and the button.

We also need a label to display the result—the length of the swing—in the user interface. Search the library for Label and drag one above the first slider such that it is at the same hierarchical level as the two sliders. The resulting storyboard structure overview should look like the following image:

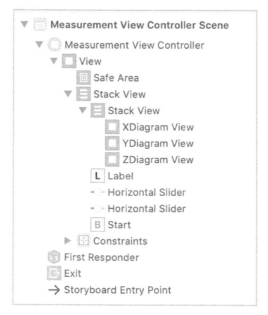

Before we connect the new user interface elements with the code, we need to adjust a few settings to make the user interface more pleasing to the eye. Select the label and open the attribute inspector using ⌥⌘5. Replace the content of the label with a hyphen and select the symbol for centering from the Alignment options. You should see the updated label in the scene of the storyboard.

Then select the outer stack view, open the attribute inspector with ⌥⌘5, and set the spacing to 5. These small changes improve the user interface a lot.

Next, select the first slider and change its value in the attribute inspector to 0. With this setting the slider thumb is all the way to the left when the view is loaded because the minimum of the slider is also set to 0. Set the value of the second slider to 1. Because the maximum of the slider is also set to 1, a value of 1 means that the slider thumb is all the way to the right when the view is loaded.

Now we can connect the label and the two sliders with the code. For the label we need an outlet (resultLabel), and for the sliders we need outlets (lowerBoundSlider and upperBoundSlider) and an action (sliderChanged). One action is enough, as we'll differentiate the two sliders using their outlets. Before you read on, think about how you would do this.

Welcome back. Did you remember how this is done? Did you try to do it yourself? If you need to remove a connection because you made a mistake, press and hold control, click the corresponding element, and then click on the x of the connection you want to remove.

Here are the steps to connect the label and the sliders with the code. Open the assistant editor using ^⌥⌘↵. Press and hold control and drag a connection from the label to below the existing properties in MeasurementViewController. Type in the name resultLabel, make sure Connection is set to Outlet, and click Connect. Do the same for the two sliders and type in the names lowerBoundSlider and upperBoundSlider, respectively. Xcode adds lines for the properties like those highlighted in the following code:

```
Sensors/MeasureSwing/MeasureSwing/MeasurementViewController.swift
  @IBOutlet var xDiagramView: DiagramView!
  @IBOutlet var yDiagramView: DiagramView!
  @IBOutlet var zDiagramView: DiagramView!
➤ @IBOutlet var resultLabel: UILabel!
➤ @IBOutlet var lowerBoundSlider: UISlider!
➤ @IBOutlet var upperBoundSlider: UISlider!
```

Now let's add the action for the sliders. Press and hold control and drag from the first slider below the last method in MeasurementViewController. Type in the name sliderChanged, make sure Connection is set to Action, change Type to UISlider, and then click Connect.

Press and hold control and drag a connection from the second slider to the name of the newly created method. Before you release the drag, Xcode should show a colored overlay on the method to inform us that this connection will go to this method rather than creating a new method. Release the drag. You can check the connection by hovering with the mouse pointer over the circle in the cutter of the code editor. Interface Builder shows the connected user interface elements with a colored overlay.

We'll use vertical lines as a marker in the diagram views. To keep track of where the marker should be positioned, we need two properties. Add the following properties to DiagramView:

```
Sensors/MeasureSwing/MeasureSwing/DiagramView.swift
var lineOnePosition: CGFloat = 0.0 {
  didSet {
    setNeedsDisplay()
  }
}
var lineTwoPosition: CGFloat = 1.0 {
  didSet {
    setNeedsDisplay()
  }
}
```

All we need to know to draw the vertical lines is the position of the line. For the position we use a value between 0 and 1 corresponding to the left and right edges of the diagram view. As we did for the dataArray property, we call setNeedsDisplay() when the property is changed. This triggers the execution of the draw(_:) method.

Next, we need to add the drawing code that uses these properties to draw vertical lines. Add the following method at the end of the class DiagramView:

```
Sensors/MeasureSwing/MeasureSwing/DiagramView.swift
func drawVerticalLine(at position: CGFloat,
                      width: CGFloat,
                      height: CGFloat) {

  let linePath = UIBezierPath()
  linePath.move(to: CGPoint(x: width * position, y: 0))
  linePath.addLine(to: CGPoint(x: width * position, y: height))

  UIColor.red.setStroke()
  linePath.lineWidth = 1
  linePath.stroke()
}
```

In this code we create an instance of UIBezierPath and set the start and end point for the path such that we get a vertical line. The position parameter is given as a fraction of the width of the diagram view. In the last three lines we set the draw color and the line width, and then we draw the vertical line.

We need to call this method within the draw(_:) method for the two marker positions. Add the following code to the end of the draw(_:) method:

```
Sensors/MeasureSwing/MeasureSwing/DiagramView.swift
drawVerticalLine(at: lineOnePosition, width: width, height: height)
drawVerticalLine(at: lineTwoPosition, width: width, height: height)
```

As we're already in the draw(_:) method in DiagramView, let's add some code that draws a zero line into the diagram. Add the following code to the end of draw(_:):

Sensors/MeasureSwing/MeasureSwing/DiagramView.swift
```
let zeroPath = UIBezierPath()
zeroPath.move(to: CGPoint(x: 0, y: y0))
zeroPath.addLine(to: CGPoint(x: width, y: y0))

UIColor.gray.setStroke()
zeroPath.lineWidth = 1
zeroPath.stroke()
```

This code draws a horizontal line from the left edge of the diagram view to the right edge at the vertical position y0.

Now that the diagram view can draw red vertical lines, open MeasurementView-Controller and add the following code in sliderChanged(_:):

Sensors/MeasureSwing/MeasureSwing/MeasurementViewController.swift
```
@IBAction func sliderChanged(_ sender: UISlider) {
➤    let value = CGFloat(sender.value)
➤    if sender == lowerBoundSlider {
➤        xDiagramView.lineOnePosition = value
➤        yDiagramView.lineOnePosition = value
➤        zDiagramView.lineOnePosition = value
➤    } else if sender == upperBoundSlider {
➤        xDiagramView.lineTwoPosition = value
➤        yDiagramView.lineTwoPosition = value
➤        zDiagramView.lineTwoPosition = value
➤    }
}
```

This code converts the value of the slider to a CGFloat and assigns it to the line position property of the diagram views. It uses the slider passed into slider-Changed(_:) to decide which line position property should be set.

Build and run the app on your iPhone, and then collect motion data and try to move the markers. If the marker doesn't move when you change the slider values, make sure that the sliders are correctly connected to the code and that the drawing code is set up correctly.

Calculating the Length from the Swing Period

The period of a pendulum is calculated using the following formula:

$$T = 2\pi \cdot \sqrt{\frac{l}{g}}$$

We can rearrange the formula to calculate the length like this:

$$l = g \cdot \left(\frac{T}{2\pi}\right)^2$$

Note that the units in these formulas are meter and second, which is usually the case in physics. The constant g in this formula stands for the gravitational acceleration, and its value is 9.81 meters per square second. T stands for the period of the swing in seconds. This means the user needs to move the markers to two adjacent maximums and we need to calculate the time difference between these two maximums. Add the following method to the end of MeasurementViewController:

Sensors/MeasureSwing/MeasureSwing/MeasurementViewController.swift

```
private func periodFromMarkers() -> TimeInterval {

  guard let firstTimestamp = xAccelerationData.first?.timestamp,
    let lastTimestamp = xAccelerationData.last?.timestamp else {

      return 0
  }
  let totalTime = lastTimestamp - firstTimestamp
  let x1 = xDiagramView.lineOnePosition
  let x2 = xDiagramView.lineTwoPosition
  return TimeInterval(x2 - x1) * totalTime
}
```

The marker positions are values between 0 and 1; they are fractions of the total recorded time. To determine the time difference between the marker positions, we need to multiply their difference by the total time frame of the recorded data.

Next, we need a method that calculates the length from the period using the formula from earlier.

Add the following code to the end of MeasurementViewController:

Sensors/MeasureSwing/MeasureSwing/MeasurementViewController.swift

```
private func lengthFrom(period: Double) -> Double {
  return 9.81 * pow(period / (2 * Double.pi), 2)
}
```

This is just the code representation of the formula for the length of the swing. The result is a Double value representing the length in meters.

With these two methods in place, we can finally calculate the length of the swing and show the result to the user. Add the following method to the end of MeasurementViewController:

```
Sensors/MeasureSwing/MeasureSwing/MeasurementViewController.swift
private func updateResultLabel() {

  let period = periodFromMarkers()
  let length = lengthFrom(period: period)

  resultLabel.text = String(format: "Length: %.3lf m", length)
}
```

This code uses the methods we've written to calculate the length of the swing and then updates the label with the result. We use a special initializer of String that allows us to format the resulting string. %.3lf tells the string that only three digits after the decimal point should be shown. We need to call this method whenever the value of a slider changes. Add the highlighted line of code to the end of sliderChanged(_:):

```
Sensors/MeasureSwing/MeasureSwing/MeasurementViewController.swift
@IBAction func sliderChanged(_ sender: UISlider) {
  let value = CGFloat(sender.value)
  if sender == lowerBoundSlider {
    xDiagramView.lineOnePosition = value
    yDiagramView.lineOnePosition = value
    zDiagramView.lineOnePosition = value
  } else if sender == upperBoundSlider {
    xDiagramView.lineTwoPosition = value
    yDiagramView.lineTwoPosition = value
    zDiagramView.lineTwoPosition = value
  }
➤   updateResultLabel()
```

Build and run the app on your iPhone and test it out. Find a playground and try to measure the length of the swing. Is the value you get plausible?

This is great. With just a few lines of code, we can now read sensor data from our iPhone and draw it on-screen. By adding the markers, we've transformed our iPhone into a measurement device as shown in the image on page 60.

With the techniques you've learned in this chapter, you can set your apps apart from many others in the App Store. You can make your apps respond to special gestures (like the one we added for the LogStore library in the appendix). By drawing on the view, you can build user interfaces that aren't possible with the built-in elements. Think about how this could improve your future apps. But be careful to not go overboard with this. Also, keep in mind that some users might not be able to perform special gestures because of disabilities. Your user interface should always have elements that can perform the action connected to the special gesture without actually requiring the special gesture. Think of the special gestures as shortcuts for actions in your app.

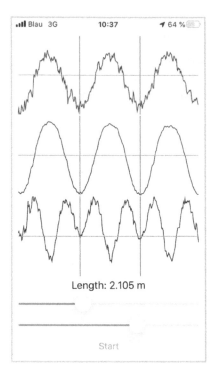

Exercises

1. Add a `smooth` function and a button to smooth the data. To smooth the data, calculate the average of each point and the two adjacent data points.

2. Add a method and a button that removes all data points below the lower marker and all data points above the upper marker. This way, you can add some kind of zoom functionality.

3. Add a time limit for the recording of data. The user should only be allowed to collect acceleration data for a few seconds because the data is drawn several times per second.

4. *(Difficult)* Try to add a method that can analyze the data to find the period without the user changing the markers.

Supermarket automatic doors open for me; therefore, I am.

> ➤ *Craig Bruce*

CHAPTER 3

Automating with Geofences

The smartphones we carry around all day would look like a magic device to someone from thirty years ago. Like a magician, we can predict the future ("Is it likely to rain in an hour?"), we can make things move ("Siri, open the front door"), and we can make something happen whenever we enter a place ("Turn heating on when I'm home").

We're used to it, but it's still fascinating, as it all seems to happen automatically. But it doesn't—underlying code gets executed because of some trigger. We can't see the trigger, and that's why it feels a bit like magic.

In this chapter we'll use such a "magic" trigger to execute our code. We'll build an app that measures how long users are outside each day without the need for any interaction from them. The app will register when the users leave their home and when they come back, and it will show a chart of the hours they spend outside each day.

The trigger we'll use is a *geofence*. A geofence is a region on a map that's coupled with an automatic action that executes when the device with the geofence enters or exits the region. In iOS, geofences are one of the few supported ways to execute code when the app in question isn't running. When the device with our app enters or exits the registered region, our app is launched in the background and can execute code for a few seconds before it's terminated.

Geofences can even be useful for apps that don't use any other location services. For example, some RSS reader and podcast apps fetch the latest items based on geofences. And years ago I used geofences to store the iPhone's battery level to estimate how long the battery would last based on the phone's usage. I'm sure you can come up with other use cases for a geofence, but first let's see how one works.

Get your magic wand and let's begin.

Setting Up the Xcode Project

Open Xcode and create a new project with the shortcut ⇧⌘N. Choose the Single View App template, click Next, and type in the product name IntoTheWild. Select SwiftUI for the user interface, click Next, and click Create.

In the app we're going to build, we'll register a region and the app will execute some code when the device enters or exits that region. Those events won't be visible in the user interface. We want to be able to check if the events actually happen and if the app does what it should. To achieve that, add the logging package we built in Appendix 1, Debugging on the Go, on page 119, to the project as described in Creating the Xcode Project, on page 1. You can find the package at https://github.com/dasdom/LogStore2.git. After you've added the package to the Xcode project, open SceneDelegate.swift and import LogStore below the existing import statements.

Geofences/IntoTheWild/IntoTheWild/SceneDelegate.swift

```
import UIKit
import SwiftUI
import LogStore
```

Then add the highlighted lines in the following code:

Geofences/IntoTheWild/IntoTheWild/SceneDelegate.swift

```
class SceneDelegate: UIResponder, UIWindowSceneDelegate {

  var window: UIWindow?
➤ var trigger: LogTrigger?

  func scene(_ scene: UIScene,
             willConnectTo session: UISceneSession,
             options connectionOptions: UIScene.ConnectionOptions) {

    let contentView = ContentView()

    if let windowScene = scene as? UIWindowScene {
      let window = UIWindow(windowScene: windowScene)
      window.rootViewController = UIHostingController(rootView: contentView)
      self.window = window
      window.makeKeyAndVisible()

➤
➤     #if DEBUG
➤     trigger = LogTrigger(in: window)
➤     #endif
    }
  }
  // ...
  // other methods
  // ...
}
```

If the app is compiled using the debug scheme, we use the log trigger to activate the trigger gesture for our logging library.

Asking for Permission

To register a geofence in iOS, we first need a location and a radius. For the location, we use the current location of the device when the user adds the geofence by tapping a button. This is much easier for us than adding a map or some other user interface element for the input of the location. As we did in Chapter 1, Drawing on Maps, on page 1, we add a class to manage the location updates.

Use the shortcut ⌘N to add a new file to the project, select the Cocoa Touch Class template, and click Next. Type in the class name LocationProvider, make it a subclass of NSObject, and click Next. In the storage location window, click Create.

We are going to access the location of the device through an instance of the class CLLocationManager defined in the framework CoreLocation. In addition we want to use the logging library we built in Appendix 1, Debugging on the Go, on page 119, to make the log accessible when we're testing our app outside. In the new file, import CoreLocation and the LogStore logging library:

Geofences/IntoTheWild/IntoTheWild/LocationProvider.swift

```
import UIKit
import CoreLocation
import LogStore
```

As the location provider will act as the delegate for a location manager, it needs to conform to the CLLocationManagerDelegate protocol. Add the CLLocationManagerDelegate protocol to the class declaration of LocationProvider so that it looks like the following code:

Geofences/IntoTheWild/IntoTheWild/LocationProvider.swift

```
class LocationProvider: NSObject,
                        CLLocationManagerDelegate {
}
```

Then add the highlighted code to LocationProvider:

Geofences/IntoTheWild/IntoTheWild/LocationProvider.swift

```
class LocationProvider: NSObject,
                        CLLocationManagerDelegate {
➤   let locationManager: CLLocationManager

➤   override init() {
➤
➤     locationManager = CLLocationManager()
➤
```

```
➤      super.init()
➤
➤      locationManager.delegate = self
➤      locationManager.requestAlwaysAuthorization()
➤    }
   }
```

In the initializer we first assign a new instance of CLLocationManager to the loca-tionManager property. Because LocationProvider is a subclass of NSObject, we need to call super.init() before we can access self. That's why we set the delegate of locationManager after the call to super.init(). The last step is to ask for permission to always request the location of the device. We need *Always authorization* because when the geofence triggers, code executes while the app isn't running. This means we need authorization from the user to access the location of the device when the app is not active.

When we call locationManager.requestAlwaysAuthorization(), iOS presents a system alert to the user to authorize access to the device location. The user can confirm, allow once, or dismiss that request. To be notified of the user's choice, we implement the delegate method locationManager(_:didChangeAuthorization:) in LocationProvider:

Geofences/IntoTheWild/IntoTheWild/LocationProvider.swift
```
func locationManager(_ manager: CLLocationManager,
                     didChangeAuthorization status:
                     CLAuthorizationStatus) {

  switch status {
  case .authorizedAlways:
    printLog("success")
  case .notDetermined:
    printLog("notDetermined")
  default:
    // FIXME: add code
    break
  }
}
```

Before the user has the chance to react to the authorization alert, this method is called with the status notDetermined and we print the word notDetermined to the log. If the user authorizes the app to always use the location, we print the word success to the log. We'll implement the default case at the end of this chapter.

Fetching the Current Location

When the user taps the button to add the geofence, our app has to fetch the current location and start to monitor a region around that location. Add the following method to LocationProvider to request the current location:

Geofences/IntoTheWild/IntoTheWild/LocationProvider.swift

```
func setHome() {
  locationManager.requestLocation()
}
```

The method requestLocation() requests the current location of the device and then stops location updates. This method is a perfect fit if you need a location only once instead of continually. The locationManager delivers the result to its delegate through the delegate method locationManager(_:didUpdateLocations:). Add the following method to LocationProvider:

Geofences/IntoTheWild/IntoTheWild/LocationProvider.swift

```
func locationManager(_ manager: CLLocationManager,
                      didUpdateLocations locations: [CLLocation]) {

  guard let location = locations.last else { return }
  printLog("location: \(location)")
}
```

From the delivered locations, we get the last one because it is the most accurate and print it to the log. We will add the code that sets the geofence later.

Before we can move on, we need to add another method because iOS throws an exception if it is not implemented by the location manager delegate. Add the following method to LocationProvider:

Geofences/IntoTheWild/IntoTheWild/LocationProvider.swift

```
func locationManager(_ manager: CLLocationManager,
                      didFailWithError error: Error) {

  printLog("locationManager didFailWithError: \(error)")
}
```

Note that this method is marked as optional in the CLLocationManagerDelegate even though the documentation states that we need to implement it. Now let's see if the request of the current location works.

Open ContentView.swift and add the following property to ContentView:

Geofences/IntoTheWild/IntoTheWild/ContentView.swift

```
struct ContentView: View {

➤   private let locationProvider = LocationProvider()

  var body: some View {
    Text("Hello, World!")
  }
}
```

Then replace the body property with the following code:

```
Geofences/IntoTheWild/IntoTheWild/ContentView.swift
var body: some View {
  VStack {
    Text("Into The Wild")
    Button("Set Home") {
      self.locationProvider.setHome()
    }
  }
}
```

In SwiftUI, you define the user interface of one view in its body property. The body is the top-level view, which can—and usually does—contain other views. In our case the body contains a vertical stack view, a VStack. This means that as in an instance of a vertical UIStackView, its content views will be arranged from top to bottom.

Pro Tip: Stacking Stack Views

 You can create sophisticated user interfaces by stacking stack views. But keep in mind that with each stack view, UIKit adds hidden layout constraints to the user interface. Views that need to be rendered quickly for optimal user experience, like table view cells, should not contain many stack views.

We add a text for the title and a button for setting the geofence to the VStack. The action of the button calls setHome() of the locationProvider.

The big advantage of SwiftUI is that we can see the user interface without running the app on the simulator. If it's not already visible, activate the canvas with the shortcut ⌥⌘↵. The canvas shows how the user interface will look when the app is running. This is much better than what you get with a storyboard because it is backed by code. If you change the code, the preview in the canvas updates instantly. But you can also change the user interface in the canvas and Xcode will add code to the body to reflect that change.

You might not see the user interface in the canvas yet. Sometimes when you change the code, the live update pauses and you have to click the Resume button at the upper right of the canvas to resume the automatic updates. Click the Resume button if it's shown and wait until the user interface is updated. The resulting Xcode window should look something like the image on page 67.

Before we can test the code we have so far by running it in the simulator, we need to add the usage descriptions for the location access requests. Apple enforces this step because the user should know how this sensitive data will be used. Most users are careful about who they let access their data.

Pro Tip: Make It Clear

A good description increases the likelihood that the user will grant the app permission to access the location. Make it clear to the user what the app does with the data. When most of the app works without that data, ask for permission to access the data only when the app needs it.

Open Info.plist and add an entry for the key NSLocationAlwaysAndWhenInUseUsageDescription with a value like "The location will be used to register the entrance and exit of the geofence." We also need to add an entry for the NSLocationWhenInUseUsageDescription key. Set the value of this entry to something like "The location will be used to register a geofence."

Build and run the app on the simulator. You should see something like the image on page 68 after the app has loaded.

Uh...this is strange. Didn't we ask for Always authorization? Why are the only options Allow While Using App, Allow Once, and Don't Allow? Did we miss something?

No, we didn't. Apple changed the access process for the location data of the user's device in iOS 13. When an app asks to always access the location of

the device, the users are asked for the access only while the app is running. Even if the user selects this option, iOS reports Always authorization to our app and we are expected to use the permission accordingly. Apple calls this *Provisional Always* authorization in the documentation. When at a later point an event occurs that requires Always authorization, iOS will ask users if they would like to upgrade the permission.

The simulator can simulate its geographic location using the Features > Location > Custom Location... menu item. Set the coordinate to a latitude of 1 and a longitude of 2, or look up the coordinates of your home address and use its latitude and longitude. Tap Allow While Using App and then tap the Set Home button we added to the user interface. Open the console in Xcode with the shortcut ⇧⌘C. In the console Xcode prints the message success and the location we set in the simulator. Nice. So far, everything works.

If you don't see the output in the console, check if you have set up the location-Provider correctly and if you called setHome() in the button action closure.

In the next section, we'll set the geofence.

Setting a Geofence

The geofence is a region we register with the location manager. Open Location-Provider.swift and add the highlighted lines at the end of the method locationManager(_:didUpdateLocations:):

Geofences/IntoTheWild/IntoTheWild/LocationProvider.swift

```
func locationManager(_ manager: CLLocationManager,
                     didUpdateLocations locations: [CLLocation]) {

  guard let location = locations.last else { return }
  printLog("location: \(location)")

➤ let region = CLCircularRegion(center: location.coordinate,
➤                               radius: 10,
➤                               identifier: "home")
➤ manager.startMonitoring(for: region)
}
```

We define a region with the location as the center, a radius of 10 meters, and an identifier. The identifier is passed into the code when the app is activated because of a geofence trigger. It can be used to distinguish between the different geofences. We're using only one geofence in this application, so the identifier isn't really necessary. Next, we tell the locationManager to monitor that region.

Pro Tip: Use Reasonable Placeholders

 Even though the identifier won't be used in our app, we should use an identifier that makes sense. We could change the app later to use more than one geofence. Or maybe we'll want to add a feature later that measures commute time. And even if we don't need the identifier in the future, it's still easier to read than a placeholder like foo.

The first part of the geofence is done. Now we need to add the action that is executed when the device enters or exits the region of the geofence. Add the following two methods to LocationProvider:

Geofences/IntoTheWild/IntoTheWild/LocationProvider.swift

```
func locationManager(_ manager: CLLocationManager,
                     didEnterRegion region: CLRegion) {

  printLog("didEnterRegion: \(String(describing: region))")
}
func locationManager(_ manager: CLLocationManager,
                     didExitRegion region: CLRegion) {

  printLog("didExitRegion: \(String(describing: region))")
}
```

These methods are declared in the CLLocationManagerDelegate. The location manager calls these methods of its delegate when the device enters or exits a monitored region. For now we print the events to the log. Let's see if the geofence works.

Build and run the app on the simulator. When the app has loaded, set the geofence by tapping the Set Home button. Then, change the simulated location in Features > Location > Custom Location… and enter 10 for Latitude and 2 for Longitude. In the console in Xcode, you should see a log entry that says the device exited the region with the identifier home. Now we need to store these events for later evaluation.

Persisting Geofence Events

To determine the time spent outside each day, we need the time the device exited and reentered the region. Let's first create an enum type that helps to differentiate between entering and exiting. Add a new file to the project using the shortcut ⌘N, choose the Swift File template, and save it as UpdateType.swift. Add the following enum to the file:

Geofences/IntoTheWild/IntoTheWild/UpdateType.swift
```
enum UpdateType : String, Codable {
  case enter
  case exit
}
```

enums in Swift let you define a type that can take a limited number of values, in this case either enter or exit. Add another Swift file, save it as RegionUpdate.swift, and add the following struct to it:

Geofences/IntoTheWild/IntoTheWild/RegionUpdate.swift
```
struct RegionUpdate : Codable {
  let date: Date
  let updateType: UpdateType
}
```

When the device enters or exits the geofence region, we want to store the current time and the type of the event. We could also store the type as a String value, but this is too fragile as it's prone to misspellings. Using an enum type helps us avoid these kinds of errors.

Pro Tip: Let the Compiler Help You

 Make your developer life easier by using data structures the compiler can check. Wrap string-based information into enums and structs. Look into tools, such as SwiftGen, that can help with generating those data structures.

Note that the struct and the enum both conform to the protocol Codable. If all the properties in a type conforming to Codable also conform to Codable, instances of that type can easily be written to a file. All basic Swift types—such as String, Date, Int, and Float—already conform to Codable.

Now we can add an array to store the region updates. Open LocationProvider and add the highlighted property below the locationManager property:

Geofences/IntoTheWild/IntoTheWild/LocationProvider.swift

```
let locationManager: CLLocationManager
➤ var regionUpdates: [RegionUpdate] = []
```

We need a method that adds the region updates to that array. Add the following method to LocationProvider.

Geofences/IntoTheWild/IntoTheWild/LocationProvider.swift

```
func addRegionUpdate(type: UpdateType) {

  let lastUpdateType = regionUpdates.last?.updateType
  if type != lastUpdateType {
    let regionUpdate = RegionUpdate(date: Date(), updateType: type)
    regionUpdates.append(regionUpdate)
  }
}
```

In this code we first check if the last element in the region updates array has a different update type than the one we want to add. We do this because we want to register only the first of the geofence events in a series of events with the same type. Technically, the event type should always alternate. But as we don't know how geofences are implemented in iOS, it's a good idea to make sure we get only the events we expect. If the new event type is different from the last, we create an instance of RegionUpdate and add it to the array.

We need to call this method when the device enters or leaves the monitored region. Add the highlighted line to locationManager(_:didEnterRegion:):

Geofences/IntoTheWild/IntoTheWild/LocationProvider.swift

```
func locationManager(_ manager: CLLocationManager,
                       didEnterRegion region: CLRegion) {

  printLog("didEnterRegion: \(String(describing: region))")

➤ addRegionUpdate(type: .enter)
}
```

Add a corresponding line to locationManager(_:didExitRegion:) with the type .exit:

Geofences/IntoTheWild/IntoTheWild/LocationProvider.swift

```
func locationManager(_ manager: CLLocationManager,
                       didExitRegion region: CLRegion) {

  printLog("didExitRegion: \(String(describing: region))")

➤ addRegionUpdate(type: .exit)
}
```

The region updates have to be stored somewhere and loaded the next time the app starts. The RegionUpdate type conforms to Codable. This means with a few lines of code, we can write the data into a *JSON* structure. JSON, short for JavaScript Object Notation, is a file format that is often used in iOS development because it's relatively compact and easy to read.

The easiest way to store the data is to write it to our app's documents directory, which is located in the app's sandbox. Files in this directory stay there until the app is deleted or until the app deletes the files itself. To manage the file URL for the storage location of the region update data, we add an extension to FileManager.

Add a new Swift file to the project using the shortcut ⌘N and save it as File-ManagerExtension.swift. Add the following extension to that file:

Geofences/IntoTheWild/IntoTheWild/FileManagerExtension.swift

```
extension FileManager {
  private static func documentsURL() -> URL {
    guard let url = FileManager.default.urls(
      for: .documentDirectory,
      in: .userDomainMask).first else {
        fatalError()
    }
    return url
  }

  static func regionUpdatesDataPath() -> URL {
    return documentsURL().appendingPathComponent("region_updates.json")
  }
}
```

The extension has two *static* methods. Static means that the methods belong to the type. To call these methods we don't need to have an instance of FileManager.

The method documentsURL() returns the file URL for the documents directory. It calls the method urls(for:in:) on the default file manager, which returns an array of file URLs. As we are asking for only one directory, we call first on the result array. If the array is empty, first returns nil; however, this should never happen because there is always a documents directory. Because our app doesn't work without the ability to store the region updates, it will crash if there's no documents directory.

In the method regionUpdatesDataPath(), we use the documents directory to create the file URL for the JSON file region_updates.json. Now that we have the file URL to store the region update data, we can write the data to the file system.

Open LocationProvider.swift and add the following method to LocationProvider:

Geofences/IntoTheWild/IntoTheWild/LocationProvider.swift

```
func writeRegionUpdates() {
  do {
    let data = try JSONEncoder().encode(regionUpdates)
    try data.write(to: FileManager.regionUpdatesDataPath(),
                   options: .atomic)
  } catch {
    printLog("error: \(error)")
  }
}
```

This code uses an instance of JSONEncoder to encode the region updates array into a Data object. Next, the data is written to the file URL in the documents directory. Note that both statements are marked with the keyword try because they can throw an error. To catch the error, we embed the code in a do catch block. If one of the statements fails, the catch closure is executed and the error is passed in. For the moment, it's enough to print the error to the console.

Pro Tip: Catch the Errors

 You can ignore the thrown error by using the try? or try! keyword. When an error is thrown, try? returns nil and try! leads to a crash. This means you throw away important information. Even if you're not planning to show the error to the user, you should still use the built-in error handling when possible or at least print the error to the console to help your future self with debugging.

When a new region update is available, we want to write the collected data to the file. Add the highlighted line to the end of the if body in addRegionUpdate(type:):

Geofences/IntoTheWild/IntoTheWild/LocationProvider.swift

```
func addRegionUpdate(type: UpdateType) {

  let lastUpdateType = regionUpdates.last?.updateType
  if type != lastUpdateType {
    let regionUpdate = RegionUpdate(date: Date(), updateType: type)
    regionUpdates.append(regionUpdate)

➤   writeRegionUpdates()
  }
}
```

When the app starts, we need to load any stored region updates. Add the following method to LocationProvider:

```
Geofences/IntoTheWild/IntoTheWild/LocationProvider.swift
func loadRegionUpdates() {
  do {
    let data = try Data(contentsOf: FileManager.regionUpdatesDataPath())
    regionUpdates = try JSONDecoder().decode([RegionUpdate].self,
                                             from: data)
  } catch {
    printLog("error: \(error)")
  }
}
```

In this code we load the JSON data from the file in the documents directory. Next we use an instance of JSONDecoder to decode the data into an array of RegionUpdates. If a type conforms to the protocol Codable, an array with elements of that type also conforms to Codable. Again, these statements can throw an error, so we have to use the keyword try and wrap the calls in a do catch block.

Note that this method will print an error when we start the app the first time because there's no file at that file URL yet.

A good time to load the stored region updates is right after creating the location provider. Add the highlighted line in init() right below super.init():

```
Geofences/IntoTheWild/IntoTheWild/LocationProvider.swift
override init() {

  locationManager = CLLocationManager()

  super.init()

➤ loadRegionUpdates()

  locationManager.delegate = self
  locationManager.requestAlwaysAuthorization()
}
```

In the next section, we'll add the code to calculate how long the user spends outside the geofence region.

Calculating the Outside Duration

To calculate the outside duration, we need a type to store the weekday and how long the user spent outside on that day. Add a new Swift file, save it as DayEntry.swift, and add the following struct to DayEntry.swift:

```
Geofences/IntoTheWild/IntoTheWild/DayEntry.swift
struct DayEntry : Hashable {
  let duration: TimeInterval
  let weekday: String
}
```

This struct conforms to Hashable because we'll iterate over an array of DayEntry objects later in this chapter, and this works only with hashable objects. *Hashing* is the process of generating a so-called hash value from some kind of input using a hash function. The hash value usually has a fixed size and is optimized to be compared quickly. You don't need to fully understand how hashing works, though—Swift manages all the heavy lifting for you.

Now we can use this type in the structure that is going to calculate the data that ContentView will show in the user interface. Add a new Swift file to the project using ⌘N and save it as DayEntriesCalculator.swift. For each day in the last seven days, we have to calculate how long the user spent outside. Let's first add a method that calculates the duration for a given date.

The method we're going to write doesn't need to store any state during the calculation. It is called with some input values and returns some output without any side effects. This means we can easily make it a type method using the static keyword. We'll call this method on the type itself without needing to create an instance of DayEntriesCalculator first.

Add the following code to DayEntriesCalculator:

Geofences/IntoTheWild/IntoTheWild/DayEntriesCalculator.swift
```
struct DayEntriesCalculator {

  static func durationFor(
    date: Date,
    from regionUpdates: [RegionUpdate]) -> TimeInterval {

    var duration = 0.0
    var enter: RegionUpdate?

    for regionUpdate in regionUpdates.reversed() {
      // calculation
    }

    return duration
  }

}
```

The method gets a date and the array with the region updates passed in as parameters. It defines a duration variable to be returned and a temporary variable to hold the last found enter event in the array. Then, it iterates over the region updates in reverse order. We use reverse order because it's easier to calculate the duration this way.

Let's see what the actual calculation looks like. Add the highlighted code in the body of the for loop:

Geofences/IntoTheWild/IntoTheWild/DayEntriesCalculator.swift

```
static func durationFor(
  date: Date,
  from regionUpdates: [RegionUpdate]) -> TimeInterval {

  var duration = 0.0
  var enter: RegionUpdate?

  for regionUpdate in regionUpdates.reversed() {
    // calculation
    if let unwrappedEnter = enter,
      regionUpdate.updateType == .exit,
      Calendar.current.isDate(date, inSameDayAs: regionUpdate.date) {

      duration += unwrappedEnter.date.timeIntervalSince(regionUpdate.date)
      enter = nil
    } else if regionUpdate.updateType == .enter {
      enter = regionUpdate
    }
  }

  return duration
}
```

This code looks a bit complicated, so let's go through it step by step. The if condition has three parts.

First, we try to unwrap the enter variable. If it's nil, unwrapping fails and the if condition is false.

Second, we check if the updateType is exit.

Third, we check if the date of the region update value matches the date passed into the method. To do so, we use the method isDate(_:inSameDayAs:) defined in the Calendar class.

If all three conditions are true, we add the time interval between the exit date and the enter date to the duration variable. Then we set enter to nil, as this enter event is now taken into account.

If one of the conditions is false, we check if the updateType is enter. In this case we store the current regionUpdate in the enter variable.

Now that we have a method that can calculate the duration for a given date, we can use it to calculate the duration for the last seven days. The result will be an array of DayEntry objects. For each object we need the duration and the name of the weekday. The easiest way to get the weekday for a given date is to use an instance of DateFormatter. Add the highlighted type property to DayEntriesCalculator:

Geofences/IntoTheWild/IntoTheWild/DayEntriesCalculator.swift

```
struct DayEntriesCalculator {
➤    static let dateFormatter: DateFormatter = {
➤      let formatter = DateFormatter()
➤      formatter.dateFormat = "EEEE"
➤      return formatter
➤    }()

    static func durationFor(
      date: Date,
      from regionUpdates: [RegionUpdate]) -> TimeInterval {

      // ...
      // method body
      // ...
    }

}
```

With these lines of code, we define a date formatter that formats a date such that only the weekday name is returned. It looks a bit strange because of the curly braces and parentheses, but it's just a closure that is called right away. This is an easy way to define something in place without the need for a setup method or an initializer. Note that we defined the property to be static to make it a type property because we want to access it from another static method.

Next, add the following method to DayEntriesCalculator:

Geofences/IntoTheWild/IntoTheWild/DayEntriesCalculator.swift

```
static func dayEntries(from regionUpdates: [RegionUpdate]) -> [DayEntry] {
  var dayEntries: [DayEntry] = []
  let now = Date()

  for i in 0..<7 {
    if let date = Calendar.current.date(byAdding: .day, value: -i, to: now) {
      let duration = durationFor(date: date, from: regionUpdates)

      let weekday = dateFormatter.string(from: date)

      dayEntries.append(DayEntry(duration: duration,
                                 weekday: weekday))
    }
  }

  return dayEntries.reversed()
}
```

In this method, we create dates for the last seven days using the method date(byAdding:value:to:) defined in Calendar. Then we use the method durationFor(date:from:) we defined previously to calculate the duration for each of these dates. We use the date formatter to get the weekday of the date.

With the duration and the weekday, we create an instance of DayEntry and add that to an array. At the end, the array contains the day entries for the last seven days, which are then returned to the caller of the method.

We could have defined the date formatter locally in the for loop, but DateFormatters are complicated objects under the hood. Creating one takes time and drains the device's battery. You should always try to reuse date formatters.

Now that we have a structure that can calculate the day entries from the region updates, let's use it in the location provider. Open LocationProvider and replace the regionUpdates property with the highlighted code:

Geofences/IntoTheWild/IntoTheWild/LocationProvider.swift

```
let locationManager: CLLocationManager
➤ var regionUpdates: [RegionUpdate] = [] {
➤   didSet {
➤     dayEntries = DayEntriesCalculator.dayEntries(from: regionUpdates)
➤   }
➤ }
➤ var dayEntries: [DayEntry] = []
```

In this code we define a property for the day entries and fill it with the calculated day entries whenever the region updates array changes.

In the next section, we'll use the framework Combine, which Apple introduced in iOS 13, to bind the duration array to the user interface. This way, the user interface will be updated whenever the day entries array changes.

Binding the User Interface and Data Using Combine

Combine was introduced by Apple at WWDC 2019. Apple states in the documentation that Combine provides a declarative Swift API for processing values over time. This is exactly what we (and most apps in general) need. We have data that has accumulated as a result of system events, and we want to process this data such that it can be shown in the user interface.

Combine declares publishers that emit data and subscribers that receive data. In our case, the location provider will publish the day entries and the user interface will subscribe to that data. Let's start with the publisher.

Open LocationProvider and replace the property declaration of dayEntries with the following line of code:

Geofences/IntoTheWild/IntoTheWild/LocationProvider.swift

```
@Published var dayEntries: [DayEntry] = []
```

By adding the attribute @Published to the property declaration of regionUpdates, we create a publisher that emits values when the array changes. Next, replace the declaration of LocationProvider with the following line of code:

```
Geofences/IntoTheWild/IntoTheWild/LocationProvider.swift
class LocationProvider: NSObject,
                        CLLocationManagerDelegate,
                        ObservableObject {
```

With this change, we make LocationProvider an observable object that emits the changed values before the @Published properties change.

To subscribe to the changes, we transform the locationProvider property into an environment variable. Replace the declaration of locationProvider in ContentView with the following line of code:

```
Geofences/IntoTheWild/IntoTheWild/ContentView.swift
@EnvironmentObject private var locationProvider: LocationProvider
```

Using @EnvironmentObject, we can pass into the class ContentView an object that can be bound to. Whenever the environment object changes, the view gets invalidated, which triggers the update of the view. Note that we removed the assignment in this line of code because this is managed by Combine.

The user interface is now bound to the day entries array. Next we'll build the SwiftUI view of a single day entry.

Presenting a Single Day Entry

A single day entry is composed of the outside duration and the first character of the weekday. In this section we'll build a SwiftUI view that shows a rectangle representing the duration relative to the maximum outside duration in the seven-day period. To start, add a new SwiftUI view using the shortcut ⌘N, select the SwiftUI View template, and click Next. Save the file as DayEntryView.

The day entry view needs the duration for that day, the maximum duration for the shown period, and the weekday. Add the following properties to DayEntryView:

```
Geofences/IntoTheWild/IntoTheWild/DayEntryView.swift
struct DayEntryView: View {
➤   let duration: TimeInterval
➤   let max: TimeInterval
➤   let weekday: String

    var body: some View {
      Text("Hello, World!")
    }
}
```

Xcode shows an error in the DayEntryView_Previews struct. Xcode uses this struct to show the preview when the canvas is activated. To make the error go away, replace the DayEntryView instance in DayEntryView_Previews struct with the highlighted line:

Geofences/IntoTheWild/IntoTheWild/DayEntryView.swift

```
struct DayEntryView_Previews: PreviewProvider {
  static var previews: some View {
➤    DayEntryView(duration: 120, max: 240, weekday: "Friday")
  }
}
```

Activate the canvas if it's not already active (with the shortcut ⌥⌘↩) and click the Resume button. In the canvas you should see the default view from the SwiftUI View template.

Replace the contents of the body property with the following code:

Geofences/IntoTheWild/IntoTheWild/DayEntryView.swift

```
struct DayEntryView: View {

  let duration: TimeInterval
  let max: TimeInterval
  let weekday: String

  var body: some View {
➤    GeometryReader { geometry in
➤      Rectangle()
➤        .frame(height: geometry.size.height *
➤          CGFloat(self.duration / self.max))
➤    }
  }
}
```

Rectangle draws a rectangle with the provided frame. The method .frame(height:) is called a *view modifier* because it modifies the view and returns the modified version. Much of the power of SwiftUI comes from the use of view modifiers.

The rectangle is embedded in a GeometryReader, which takes all available space and passes an instance of GeometryProxy into its closure. The geometry proxy holds information about the available space in the view. We use it here to calculate the height for the rectangle based on the maximal value. If the maximum duration is 240 and the duration is 120, the rectangle's height is set to half of the available height.

Click the Resume button to update the canvas. You should see a black rectangle in the middle of the screen that spans the whole width of the simulated screen.

The user interface looks better when the rectangle is pinned to the bottom of the screen. Add the highlighted lines of code to the body:

Geofences/IntoTheWild/IntoTheWild/DayEntryView.swift

```
struct DayEntryView: View {

  let duration: TimeInterval
  let max: TimeInterval
  let weekday: String

  var body: some View {
    GeometryReader { geometry in
➤     VStack {
➤       Spacer(minLength: 0)
        Rectangle()
          .frame(height: geometry.size.height *
            CGFloat(self.duration / self.max))
➤     }
      }
    }
}
```

We have embedded the rectangle in a VStack and added a Spacer with a minLength of 0 above it. This way, we move the rectangle to the bottom of the screen.

You don't have to reindent the code yourself; Xcode can help you with this. Use the shortcut ⌘A to select all the lines in the file and then press ^I to reindent them.

We want to add the number of hours and minutes to each rectangle because this is the main information in our app. To format the duration accordingly, add the following method to DayEntryView:

Geofences/IntoTheWild/IntoTheWild/DayEntryView.swift

```
func durationString(from duration: TimeInterval) -> String {

  let formatter = DateComponentsFormatter()
  formatter.allowedUnits = [.hour, .minute]
  formatter.unitsStyle = .abbreviated

  return formatter.string(from: duration) ?? ""
}
```

In this code we use a DateComponentFormatter to format the time interval into a string. We set the unitStyle to abbreviated because this results in a compact string perfect for being displayed in our user interface. A time interval of 4,260 seconds results in the formatted string "1h 11m."

Now we can add that string to the rectangles. In SwiftUI, we can stack views on top of each other using a ZStack. Add the highlighted lines in the following code to the body:

Geofences/IntoTheWild/IntoTheWild/DayEntryView.swift
```swift
struct DayEntryView: View {

  let duration: TimeInterval
  let max: TimeInterval
  let weekday: String

  var body: some View {
    GeometryReader { geometry in
      VStack {
        Spacer(minLength: 0)
➤       ZStack(alignment: .top) {
          Rectangle()
            .frame(height: geometry.size.height *
              CGFloat(self.duration / self.max))
➤         if self.duration > 0 {
➤           Text(self.durationString(from: self.duration))
➤             .foregroundColor(.white)
➤             .font(.footnote)
➤         }
➤       }
        }
      }
    }
  }
}
```

If the duration is greater than zero, we add text with the text color white and the font size footnote to the ZStack. We use the font size footnote because we want to fit seven day entries onto the small screen of an iPhone SE and still keep the text readable. Later, when we change the app to support dark mode, we'll adjust the text color. Click the Resume button to update the canvas.

Nice. We are nearly finished with the day entry view. The only task remaining is the abbreviation of the weekday below the rectangle. Again we'll embed the existing structure into a stack view. Replace the existing body content with the following code:

Geofences/IntoTheWild/IntoTheWild/DayEntryView.swift
```swift
struct DayEntryView: View {

  let duration: TimeInterval
  let max: TimeInterval
  let weekday: String

  var body: some View {
➤   VStack {
      GeometryReader { geometry in
        VStack {
          Spacer(minLength: 0)
```

```
        ZStack(alignment: .top) {
          Rectangle()
            .frame(height: geometry.size.height *
              CGFloat(self.duration / self.max))
          if self.duration > 0 {
            Text(self.durationString(from: self.duration))
              .foregroundColor(.white)
              .font(.footnote)
          }
        }
      }
    }
  }
➤     Text(String(self.weekday.first ?? " "))
➤   }
  }
}
```

We have embedded the GeometryReader and all its contents in a VStack and added a text at the bottom. If the canvas doesn't update by itself, click the Resume button. This looks good enough. If you'd like to play around with colors and modifiers, go for it—experiment a bit with SwiftUI.

Are you finished with your experiments for now? Then let's see how the user interface looks in dark mode.

The preview in the canvas on the right side is not limited to one screen. We can add many different screens showing different screen sizes and user interface modes. To see how to add a preview for dark mode, replace the contents of previews in DayEntryView_Previews at the end of the file with the highlighted code:

Geofences/IntoTheWild/IntoTheWild/DayEntryView.swift
```
struct DayEntryView_Previews: PreviewProvider {
  static var previews: some View {
➤     Group {
➤       DayEntryView(duration: 120, max: 240, weekday: "Friday")
➤       DayEntryView(duration: 20640, max: 30000, weekday: "Tuesday")
➤         .background(Color(UIColor.systemBackground))
➤         .environment(\.colorScheme, .dark)
➤     }
  }
}
```

This code adds a dark mode preview to the canvas as shown in the image on page 84.

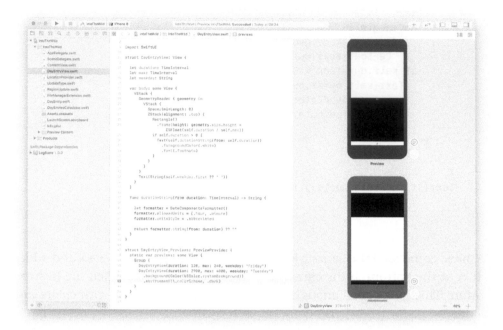

Note that we have embedded the previews into a Group. This is necessary because the top-level element in previews needs to be just one element. The user interface mode is set using the environment modifier with the key path \.colorScheme.

As you can see in the canvas, the day view doesn't support dark mode yet. The text we stacked on top of the rectangle is not visible because we set the text color to white. The color of the rectangle is changed in dark mode automatically. But if you set the color of the rectangle to a custom value, you'll need to adapt it for dark mode.

Let's add a custom color set to fix the user interface. Open Assets.xcassets and add a color set by selecting the Xcode menu item Editor > Add Assets > New Color Set. Change the name of the color set to durationTextColor.

Next, open the attributes inspector using the shortcut ⌥⌘4 and set Appearances to Any, Dark. Xcode adds color selectors for Any Appearance and for Dark Appearance. Select the color for Dark Appearance and change it in the attribute inspector to a dark gray. Now select the color for Any Appearance and change it to a light gray. The resulting color set should look like the image on page 85.

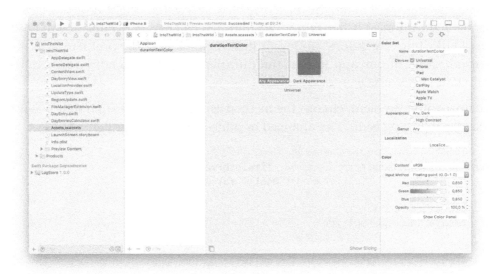

Open DayEntryView again and change the highlighted line in the following code:

```
Geofences/IntoTheWild/IntoTheWild/DayEntryView.swift
GeometryReader { geometry in
  VStack {
    Spacer(minLength: 0)
    ZStack(alignment: .top) {
      Rectangle()
        .frame(height: geometry.size.height *
          CGFloat(self.duration / self.max))
      if self.duration > 0 {
        Text(self.durationString(from: self.duration))
          .foregroundColor(Color("durationTextColor"))
          .font(.footnote)
      }
    }
  }
}
```

Click the Resume button. The text is now visible in both light and dark mode.

Making the Day Entry Accessible

Apple works hard to make its products accessible for people with disabilities. One of the accessibility features built into iOS is the screen reader VoiceOver. All UIKit controls automatically work with VoiceOver. But sometimes we have to add a few lines of code to make our apps accessible for visually impaired users.

In this section we'll make the day entry view accessible. Right now VoiceOver reads a duration of 2 hours and 25 minutes as "two h twenty-five m." We would like it to say "hours" and "minutes" instead. Another problem with the current state of our app is that the duration and the weekday seem to be unrelated for VoiceOver.

To fix the first problem, change the method durationString(from:) such that it looks like the following code. The changed or added lines are highlighted.

Geofences/IntoTheWild/IntoTheWild/DayEntryView.swift
```
func durationString(from duration: TimeInterval,
                    forVoiceOver: Bool = false) -> String {

  if duration < 1 {
    return "no time outside"
  }

  let formatter = DateComponentsFormatter()
  formatter.allowedUnits = [.hour, .minute]

  if forVoiceOver {
    formatter.unitsStyle = .full
  } else {
    formatter.unitsStyle = .abbreviated
  }

  return formatter.string(from: duration) ?? ""
}
```

If the method is called with forVoiceOver: true, the returned string is optimized for VoiceOver users. In this case we also return a string if the duration is zero, because this feels more natural for VoiceOver users.

Next, add the following method to DayEntryView:

Geofences/IntoTheWild/IntoTheWild/DayEntryView.swift
```
func voiceOverGroupString(for duration: TimeInterval) -> String {
  let duration = durationString(from: duration, forVoiceOver: true)
  return "\(duration) on \(weekday)"
}
```

This method creates and returns the string we want to add for VoiceOver users when they select a day entry.

To group the duration and the weekday for VoiceOver, add the following view modifier to the top-level VStack in the body of DayEntryView:

```
Geofences/IntoTheWild/IntoTheWild/DayEntryView.swift
var body: some View {
  VStack {
    // ...
    // views
    // ...
  }
  .accessibilityElement(children: .ignore)
  .accessibility(label: Text(voiceOverGroupString(for: duration)))
}
```

The first modifier disables accessibility for the children of the VStack. We do this because we want to provide an accessibility label for the group. The second modifier adds the text that VoiceOver will speak when the user selects this VStack.

This is all we have to do to make this app usable for visually impaired users. But not only for them—many other accessibility features work automatically when VoiceOver works because they use the same underlying information.

The day entry view is now finished. Next we'll combine several day entry views to show the outside duration of the last seven days.

Combining Day Entry Views for a Week Overview

The day entry view needs the maximum duration to provide the correct scaling to its rectangle. Before we can show the day entry views for the last seven days, though, we need to calculate the maximum duration of these entries. Open LocationProvider and add the following property:

```
Geofences/IntoTheWild/IntoTheWild/LocationProvider.swift
var max: TimeInterval = 1
```

To calculate the maximum, replace the dayEntries property declaration with the following code:

```
Geofences/IntoTheWild/IntoTheWild/LocationProvider.swift
@Published var dayEntries: [DayEntry] = []  {
  didSet {
    max = dayEntries.reduce(1.0, { result, nextDayEntry in
      Swift.max(result, nextDayEntry.duration)
    })
  }
}
```

This looks more complicated than it is. We use the reduce() method defined on Collection, which uses an initial value (in our case, 1.0) and iterates over all elements in the collection. For each element the closure gets executed. The first parameter of the closure is the result of the last iteration, and the second parameter is the current element in the collection.

In the closure we call the global function Swift.max(_:_:). The word Swift tells the compiler that we mean the global max(_:_:) function. We need this here because we have a property with the same name, so the compiler could get confused otherwise.

The reduce() method iterates over the day entries array and finds the maximum duration. If the day entries array is empty, it returns 1.0. We choose 1.0 instead of 0.0 as the minimum value here because we'll divide by this value in the next step, and dividing by zero is not allowed.

Now we can add the day entries to the main user interface. Open ContentView and add the highlighted lines to the body contents:

```
Geofences/IntoTheWild/IntoTheWild/ContentView.swift
var body: some View {
  VStack {
    Text("Into The Wild")
    Button("Set Home") {
      self.locationProvider.setHome()
    }
➤   HStack(alignment: .bottom, spacing: 2) {
➤     ForEach(self.locationProvider.dayEntries, id: \.self) { value in
➤       DayEntryView(duration: value.duration,
➤                    max: self.locationProvider.max,
➤                    weekday: value.weekday)
➤     }
➤   }
➤   .padding()
  }
➤ .background(Color(UIColor.systemBackground))
}
```

In this code we iterate over all day entries, create day entry views from them, and put those into an HStack. This works only because we made DayEntry conform to Hashable. In addition, we set the background color of the main VStack to Color(UIColor.systemBackground)) to make the app work in both light and dark mode.

The preview in ContentView doesn't work right now. To make it work again, replace the ContentView_Previews struct with the following code:

```
Geofences/IntoTheWild/IntoTheWild/ContentView.swift
struct ContentView_Previews: PreviewProvider {

  static var locationProvider: LocationProvider = {
    let locationProvider = LocationProvider()
    locationProvider.dayEntries = [
      DayEntry(duration: 20640, weekday: "Monday"),
      DayEntry(duration: 2580, weekday: "Tuesday" ),
      DayEntry(duration: 12000, weekday: "Wednesday"),
      DayEntry(duration: 1200, weekday: "Thursday"),
      DayEntry(duration: 2220, weekday: "Friday"),
      DayEntry(duration: 19920, weekday: "Saturday"),
      DayEntry(duration: 18000, weekday: "Sunday"),
    ]
    return locationProvider
  }()

  static var previews: some View {
    Group {
      ContentView()
        .environmentObject(locationProvider)
      ContentView()
        .environmentObject(locationProvider)
        .environment(\.colorScheme, .dark)
    }
  }
}
```

First we define a location provider for the preview and fill it with seven day entries. We add a group with two previews, one for light mode (the default) and one for dark mode. Then we set the location provider as an environment object for the content view preview. Unfortunately, this still isn't enough to make the preview work. We also have to set the environment in the setup of the app.

Open SceneDelegate and add the highlighted line in scene(_:willConnectTo:options:):

```
Geofences/IntoTheWild/IntoTheWild/SceneDelegate.swift
func scene(_ scene: UIScene,
           willConnectTo session: UISceneSession,
           options connectionOptions: UIScene.ConnectionOptions) {

  let contentView = ContentView()
➤   .environmentObject(LocationProvider())

  if let windowScene = scene as? UIWindowScene {
    let window = UIWindow(windowScene: windowScene)
    window.rootViewController = UIHostingController(rootView: contentView)
    self.window = window
    window.makeKeyAndVisible()
```

```
    #if DEBUG
    trigger = LogTrigger(in: window)
    #endif
  }
}
```

With this code we set the environment of the content view. Go back to ContentView and click the Resume button. If you see a Try Again button rather than Resume, click it instead.

The canvas should show the user interface with the outside times. If there's an error in the code, try to fix it according to what Xcode tells you about the error. If you still can't get the code to work, delete the lines with errors until it works and then repeat this section to add the code again.

Handling Wrong Authorization

When the user doesn't authorize our app to always use the location data, the app doesn't work. In this case we should present an alert to the user that the app can't deliver the promised functionality. As we did for the day entries data, we use Combine to bind the user interface to the information if the correct authorization is given. Open LocationProvider and add the following property:

Geofences/IntoTheWild/IntoTheWild/LocationProvider.swift
```
@Published var wrongAuthorization = false
```

This property keeps track of the authorization status. We need to set it to true when the authorization status is not authorizedAlways. Add the highlighted line in the following code to locationManager(_:didChangeAuthorization:):

Geofences/IntoTheWild/IntoTheWild/LocationProvider.swift
```
func locationManager(_ manager: CLLocationManager,
                     didChangeAuthorization status:
                     CLAuthorizationStatus) {
  switch status {
  case .authorizedAlways:
    printLog("success")
  case .notDetermined:
    printLog("notDetermined")
  default:
➤   wrongAuthorization = true
  }
}
```

Next we need the code that presents the alert to the user when Not Always authorization is granted. Open ContentView and add the highlighted modifier to the outer VStack:

```
Geofences/IntoTheWild/IntoTheWild/ContentView.swift
    .background(Color(UIColor.systemBackground))
➤   .alert(isPresented: $locationProvider.wrongAuthorization) {
➤     Alert(title: Text("Not authorized"),
➤           message: Text("Open settings and authorize."),
➤           primaryButton: .default(Text("Settings"), action: {
➤             UIApplication.shared.open(
➤               URL(string: UIApplication.openSettingsURLString)!)
➤           }),
➤           secondaryButton: .default(Text("OK")))
➤   }
```

The modifier .alert(…) presents an alert to the user when the bound value of
the first parameter becomes true. The alert itself is defined in the closure of
the alert modifier. In this case we define an alert with a title, a message, and
two buttons. For the first button we add an action that opens the app settings
in the iOS Settings app. The user can then change the authorization to make
the app work again.

Our app is finished. Build and run it on your iPhone and see how much time
you spend outside. After you've used the app for a few days, you should see
something like the following image:

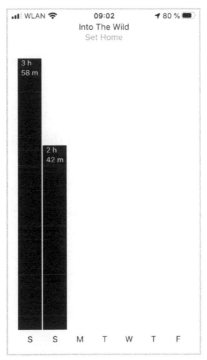

As you can see from my data, I work from home.

Things to Remember When Working with Geofences

When you're working with geofences, there are a few things you need to keep in mind.

Hard limit of twenty geofences

There is a hard limit of twenty for the number of geofences an app can register because regions are shared resources that rely on specific hardware capabilities. If you need to monitor more regions, the documentation recommends registering only regions that are close to the user's current location and updating that list when the user moves.

Delay

After crossing the boundary, the user has to travel a minimum distance and remain on the same side of the boundary for at least twenty seconds before the system calls the delegate methods. With this implementation, Apple reduces the number of spurious calls to the delegate.

Background App Refresh

When Background App Refresh is disabled, geofences won't trigger the wake-up of your app. The user needs to explicitly launch the app to resume the delivery of location-related events.

iBeacons

Instead of circular regions, you can register iBeacon regions. Apart from the trigger, they work the same way.

Exercises

1. Add a label to the user interface showing the total duration spent outside in the displayed seven-day period.

2. Change the colors to make the app more appealing.

3. Add a feature that lets the user switch to week view, where each rectangle represents the data for one week.

Reality is merely an illusion, albeit a very persistent one.

➢ *Albert Einstein*

CHAPTER 4

Sharing Augmented Reality

As kids, we used to have scavenger hunts. One team gets a head start and draws arrow hints on the ground. The second team then finds the first team by following the arrows. Sometimes the arrows point in two directions, so the second team has to try both directions to find the correct one.

Today, kids hunt Pokemon in *Pokemon Go*. The Pokemon in the mobile game are attached to a real-world location. When the players arrive at that location, they can catch the Pokemon with their mobile device.

Pokemon Go is like the scavenger hunts we used to have back in the day, but the focus is more on the Pokemon than on the teams hunting each other. Let's try to combine aspects of *Pokemon Go* with the scavenger hunts we had before mobile devices came along. In this chapter we'll create an app that lets a player draw text on the ground using ARKit. Another player will then be able to find the drawn text using only the app.

This might not sound like anything special, but under the hood, it's quite cool. ARKit creates a map of the surroundings where the player adds the text. When another player uses an iPhone to scan the ground again, ARKit recognizes that it already has mapped this location and shows the text from the first player.

With these features of ARKit, you can build collaborative augmented reality apps. Two or more people can share the same augmented reality using different devices.

For this app we'll use a storyboard for the user interface.

Let the hunting begin.

Setting Up an Augmented Reality App

Open Xcode, create a new app using the shortcut ⇧⌘N, and select the Augmented Reality App template. Type in ScavengerHunt for the Product Name, select SpriteKit for the Content Technology, and click Next. Select a location on your Mac for the project and click Create.

Have a look at the created project. We are using SpriteKit to render our content into the augmented reality view (*AR view* for short). SpriteKit is a framework that allows us to add and manage two-dimensional objects that behave like real objects. It is often used for casual games like side scrollers. Because we are using SpriteKit, Xcode adds files for the SpriteKit scene. The Scene.sks is an archive of the scenes content—we won't change it in this project. Instead, we'll use the Scene.swift file to implement the placement of the text.

Let's see what the app looks like before we change anything. Build and run the app on your iPhone, move your device, and tap the screen. You should see the camera view with an added alien emoji at the locations where you tapped the screen. It should look something like the following image:

To see how this works, open Scene.swift in Xcode. The method touchesBegan(_:with:) adds instances of ARAnchor to the session of the SpriteKit scene.

The actual placement of the alien sprites is handled in ViewController in the delegate method view(_:nodeFor:).

Now let's add our logging library to the project to make outside testing easier.

Adding Our Logging Library

Select the Xcode menu item File > Swift Packages > Add Package Dependency and paste in the URL of your package from one of the supported hosting services. If you didn't post your package to one of the services, you can use mine.[1] Add the package as you did in the previous chapters.

Previously we had to set up the trigger window in the SceneDelegate of the project. Augmented reality apps don't have a scene delegate, so instead we'll add the trigger to the AppDelegate. Open AppDelegate.swift and add the highlighted lines in the following code:

```
ARKit/ScavengerHunt/AppDelegate.swift
import UIKit
➤ import LogStore

@UIApplicationMain
class AppDelegate: UIResponder, UIApplicationDelegate {

  var window: UIWindow?
➤ var trigger: LogTrigger?

  func application(
    _ application: UIApplication,
    didFinishLaunchingWithOptions launchOptions:
    [UIApplication.LaunchOptionsKey: Any]?) -> Bool {

➤   #if DEBUG
➤   trigger = LogTrigger(in: window)
➤   #endif

    return true
  }
  // ...
  // other methods
  // ...
}
```

This code should be quite familiar to you now. As a refresher, this code defines and sets up an instance of LogTrigger when we build the app in the debug configuration. The log trigger allows the user to perform a special gesture with the iPhone to show the log in the running app without using Xcode.

---

1. https://github.com/dasdom/LogStore2.git

Now we'll move on to the screen that shows the distance to the text location.

Getting and Managing Location Updates

As long as the players are more than 10 meters away from the place where the text is drawn, they should see a screen showing the distance to that location. Using this information, they have to find the text's location. As soon as the players get within 10 meters of the text, they will see the AR view on their screen and they can search for the text.

As we did in the previous chapters, let's add a class that manages the location updates from the GPS sensor. Use the shortcut ⌘N to add a new Cocoa Touch class, call it LocationProvider, and make it a subclass of NSObject.

Import CoreLocation and the LogStore logging library into LocationProvider.swift:

ARKit/ScavengerHunt/LocationProvider.swift
```
import UIKit
import CoreLocation
import LogStore
```

Next, add or change the highlighted code that initializes and sets up a location manager:

ARKit/ScavengerHunt/LocationProvider.swift
```
class LocationProvider: NSObject, CLLocationManagerDelegate {

  private let locationManager: CLLocationManager

  override init() {

    locationManager = CLLocationManager()

    super.init()

    locationManager.delegate = self
    locationManager.requestWhenInUseAuthorization()
  }
}
```

If you've worked through the other chapters, this code should be quite familiar to you. The location manager delivers the location updates to its delegate. We'll display the distance to the text location only when the app is running. This means we need to ask the user only for When in Use authorization.

Note that we added the protocol CLLocationManagerDelegate to the class declaration because the location provider acts as the delegate for the location manager.

The call locationManager.requestWhenInUseAuthorization() triggers the request shown to the users. To react to the user's selection, add the following method to LocationManager:

ARKit/ScavengerHunt/LocationProvider.swift

```swift
func locationManager(_ manager: CLLocationManager,
                     didChangeAuthorization status: CLAuthorizationStatus) {

  switch status {
  case .authorizedWhenInUse:
    printLog("success")
  default:
    // ToDo: implement
    break
  }
}
```

This method prints success to the console when the user grants the request. Implement the other case as an exercise. You can find the other cases when you open the developer documentation with the shortcut ⇧⌘0 and search for CLAuthorizationStatus. Think about what the app might look like without access to the current location. If you don't know how to make it usable in this case, inform the users of that.

Unfortunately, you can't ask for the authorization again. The users need to open the iOS settings and update the authorization themselves if they change their mind. You can redirect the user to the app settings with the following code:

```swift
UIApplication.shared.open(URL(string: UIApplication.openSettingsURLString)!)
```

The property locationManager is defined as private, which means that it is accessible only from within this class. Other classes don't need to know where the location updates originate from. To make it possible to start and stop the location events from outside of this class, add the following code to Location-Provider:

ARKit/ScavengerHunt/LocationProvider.swift

```swift
func start() {
  locationManager.startUpdatingLocation()
}

func stop() {
  locationManager.stopUpdatingLocation()
}
```

These methods call the corresponding methods on locationManager.

Pro Tip: Hide Implementation Detail

 Hide implementation details from other parts of the code. This way, you can change how the class or structure works without breaking the app. Try to build the interface of your classes and structures so they don't need to change when the implementation changes.

In Chapter 1, Drawing on Maps, on page 1, we used a closure to propagate the location updates to the user interface. In this chapter, we'll use Combine for this task. Import Combine into LocationProvider.swift:

ARKit/ScavengerHunt/LocationProvider.swift
```
import UIKit
import CoreLocation
import LogStore
import Combine
```

Next, add the highlighted property below the locationManager property:

ARKit/ScavengerHunt/LocationProvider.swift
```
  private let locationManager: CLLocationManager
➤ @Published var lastLocation: CLLocation?
```

With the @Published property wrapper, we create a publisher for that property. Whenever the location manager delivers a new location, we assign it to this property. Add the following method to LocationProvider:

ARKit/ScavengerHunt/LocationProvider.swift
```
func locationManager(_ manager: CLLocationManager,
                     didUpdateLocations locations: [CLLocation]) {

  lastLocation = locations.last
}
```

To make this code work, we need to add the usage description into Info.plist. Open Info.plist and add an entry with the key NSLocationWhenInUseUsageDescription and the text "The location will be used to show the distance to a stored location." That's all for the LocationProvider. Next, we'll implement the view controller that will show the distance to the text location.

Implementing the Distance Screen

Add a new Cocoa Touch class to the project, call it DistanceViewController, and make it a subclass of UIViewController.

Open Main.storyboard and drag a view controller from the library (⇧⌘L) to the storyboard. Select the new view controller in the structure area and open the identity inspector using the shortcut ⌥⌘4. Set the class of the view controller to DistanceViewController. Next, open the attributes inspector with the shortcut ⌥⌘5 and select the check box for Is Initial View Controller. With this change, iOS shows an instance of this view controller when the app launches.

We want to show the distance in meters in a label. Drag a UILabel from the library to the scene of the DistanceViewController. Pin the label left and right with a padding of 20 points to the super view, as shown in the following image:

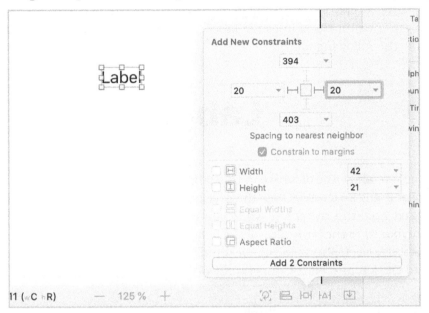

Click the button Add 2 Constraints. Don't pin the view to the top or the bottom. Next, with the label selected, click the Align button and select the check box for Vertically in Container, as in the following image:

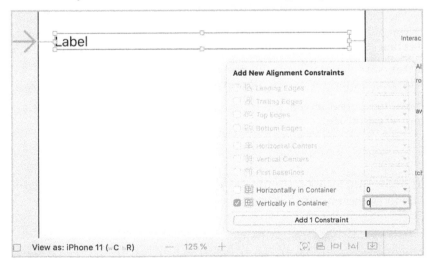

Then click the button Add 1 Constraint. Those three constraints are enough to center the label vertically, spanning from left to right of the view. Now let's improve the appearance of the label.

Select the label and open the attributes inspector with the shortcut ⌥⌘5. Change the font to System Black 35 and select the symbol for centering from the Alignment options. Finally, set the number in the Lines text field to 0. This sets the supported line number of the label to 0, which means that there's no limit to the number of lines the label can show. The resulting label should look like the following image:

To be able to show the distance in this label, we need to connect it to the view controller using an IBOutlet. Open the assistant editor with the shortcut ⌃⌥⌘↩. Press and hold the `control` key while you drag a connection from the label in the storyboard to the beginning of the DistanceViewController class. Type the name distanceLabel, select Strong in the picker at the bottom, make sure Connection is set to Outlet, and click Connect. Xcode adds the following code:

ARKit/ScavengerHunt/DistanceViewController.swift
```
@IBOutlet var distanceLabel: UILabel!
```

We want to update the user interface when a new location event is delivered to the location provider. To achieve that, the DistanceViewController needs to hold a reference to an instance of LocationProvider:

ARKit/ScavengerHunt/DistanceViewController.swift
```
class DistanceViewController: UIViewController {

  @IBOutlet var distanceLabel: UILabel!
➤ private let locationProvider = LocationProvider()

  override func viewDidLoad() {
    super.viewDidLoad()

  }
}
```

To start delivering location events to the location provider, add the highlighted line of code to the end of viewDidLoad():

ARKit/ScavengerHunt/DistanceViewController.swift

```
override func viewDidLoad() {
  super.viewDidLoad()

  locationProvider.start()
}
```

Next, we need to subscribe to updates to the lastLocation property of Location-Provider. Import Combine below the existing import statement. Let's also add our logging library because we'll need it later in this section:

ARKit/ScavengerHunt/DistanceViewController.swift

```
import UIKit
import Combine
import LogStore
```

Then add this property for the subscription below the locationProvider property:

ARKit/ScavengerHunt/DistanceViewController.swift

```
private var subscription: AnyCancellable?
```

Next, add the highlighted code to viewDidLoad():

ARKit/ScavengerHunt/DistanceViewController.swift

```
class DistanceViewController: UIViewController {

  @IBOutlet var distanceLabel: UILabel!
  private let locationProvider = LocationProvider()
  private var subscription: AnyCancellable?

  override func viewDidLoad() {
    super.viewDidLoad()

    locationProvider.start()

    subscription = locationProvider.$lastLocation
      .sink(receiveValue: updateUI)
  }
}
```

With this code, we subscribe to updates to lastLocation in the location provider. The changes are processed by a .sink statement, which passes the received values to a closure or a method provided in the parameter. We use a yet-to-be-written method, updateUI(). Let's add this method now.

First, import Core Location into DistanceViewController.swift.

ARKit/ScavengerHunt/DistanceViewController.swift

```
import UIKit
import Combine
import LogStore
import CoreLocation
```

Then add the following method to DistanceViewController:

ARKit/ScavengerHunt/DistanceViewController.swift
```swift
func updateUI(for location: CLLocation?) {

  guard let location = location else {
    return
  }

  let coordinate = location.coordinate
  distanceLabel.text = String(format: "%.6lf, %.6lf",
                              coordinate.latitude,
                              coordinate.longitude)
}
```

The lastLocation property in LocationProvider is an optional. As a result, the delivered updates are also optional values. Before we try to update the user interface using the new value, we check if the value is nonoptional. If the value is nil, we do nothing for the moment. Maybe later when we use the app, we'll get a better idea of what to do in this case.

Next, we use the coordinate of the unwrapped location to populate the distance label with the latitude and longitude of the last registered location. The latitude and longitude are of type CLLocationDegrees, which is a type alias for Double. This means that when we try to print the values, they'll have many digits after the decimal point. To limit the number of digits printed to the label, we use a formatted string with the format specifier %.6lf. The percent sign tells the compiler that this is the position where the value should be inserted, .6 means that it should print six digits after the decimal point, and lf stands for Double.

Build and run the app on the simulator. In the app menu of the running simulator, select Features > Location > Custom Location.... In the window Xcode presents, change the Latitude to 1 and the Longitude to 2 and click OK.

At this point, the app doesn't show the distance to some location; it just shows the current coordinate. To show a distance, we need to store a location when the user taps a button. Add the highlighted property below the existing properties:

ARKit/ScavengerHunt/DistanceViewController.swift
```swift
@IBOutlet var distanceLabel: UILabel!
private let locationProvider = LocationProvider()
private var subscription: AnyCancellable?
private var storedLocation: CLLocation?
```

Now let's add a button to assign this new property.

Open Main.storyboard and drag a button from the library to the bottom of the DistanceViewController scene. Pin the button to the bottom of the screen with a distance of 10 points and align it horizontally in its container. Set the title of the button to Set Anchor. When you're finished with these changes, the button should look like the following image:

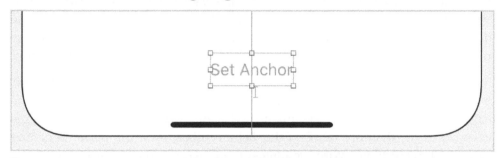

Next, open the assistant editor (if you don't remember the shortcut, look it up in Xcode). Press and hold the `control` key and drag a connection from the button below the last method in DistanceViewController. Type in the name setAnchor and change Type to UIButton, make sure Connection is set to Action, and click Connect.

Add the highlighted line of code to the body of the new method setAnchor(_:):

ARKit/ScavengerHunt/DistanceViewController.swift
```
@IBAction func setAnchor(_ sender: UIButton) {
    storedLocation = locationProvider.lastLocation
}
```

With this code, we assign the current value of the lastLocation property of the location provider to the new property. Next we need to update the code that updates the distance label. Add the highlighted lines to the body of the updateUI(for:) method:

ARKit/ScavengerHunt/DistanceViewController.swift
```
func updateUI(for location: CLLocation?) {

    guard let location = location else {
        return
    }

    if let storedLocation = storedLocation {

        let distance = location.distance(from: storedLocation)
        distanceLabel.text = String(format: "%.2lf m", distance)

    } else {
        let coordinate = location.coordinate
        distanceLabel.text = String(format: "%.6lf, %.6lf",
                                    coordinate.latitude,
                                    coordinate.longitude)

    }
}
```

If the stored location is not nil, we calculate its distance to the location passed into updateUI(for:) and use the distance to update the label.

Build and run the app on the simulator and click the Set Anchor button. Next, set the latitude of the custom location to 1.0001. The label changes to show the distance to the stored location. If it doesn't work, make sure that the button is properly connected and that the location is stored when you tab the button.

Nice—the distance screen works. Before we move on, let's improve the user experience. When using this screen, the players need to know if they are getting closer to the coordinate of the augmented reality feature. This information is encoded in the distance label—if the distance decreases, the player is getting closer to the coordinate. With a few lines of code, we can make this more obvious.

First, add the following property to DistanceViewController:

ARKit/ScavengerHunt/DistanceViewController.swift
```
private var lastDistance: CLLocationDistance = 0
```

Next, add the highlighted code in updateUI(for:):

ARKit/ScavengerHunt/DistanceViewController.swift
```
func updateUI(for location: CLLocation?) {

  guard let location = location else {
    return
  }

  if let storedLocation = storedLocation {

    let distance = location.distance(from: storedLocation)
    distanceLabel.text = String(format: "%.2lf m", distance)

➤    if lastDistance < distance {
➤      view.backgroundColor = .red
➤    } else if lastDistance > distance {
➤      view.backgroundColor = .green
➤    }
➤
➤    lastDistance = distance
  } else {
    let coordinate = location.coordinate
    distanceLabel.text = String(format: "%.6lf, %.6lf",
                                coordinate.latitude,
                                coordinate.longitude)
  }
}
```

When the distance increases, we change the background color to red, and when it decreases, we change it to green. Build and run the app on the simulator and simulate a few custom locations in the feature menu item of the simulator. Verify that the background color changes accordingly.

It works, but you might want to use better colors for the background. The default red and green colors in Swift are not very pleasing to the eye.

Right now the stored location is stored only as long as the app is executing. As CLLocation conforms to NSSecureCoding, we can convert an instance of CLLocation to an instance of Data and vice versa. But first we need a file URL where we can write the data to disk.

Create a new Swift file, call it FileManagerExtension.swift, and add the following code to it:

```
ARKit/ScavengerHunt/FileManagerExtension.swift
extension FileManager {
  private static func documentsURL() -> URL {
    guard let url = FileManager.default.urls(
      for: .documentDirectory,
      in: .userDomainMask).first else {
        fatalError()
    }
    return url
  }

  static func locationURL() -> URL {
    return documentsURL().appendingPathComponent("location")
  }

}
```

The method documentsURL() returns the file URL of the documents directory. Every iOS app has this directory in its sandbox. The second method uses the first method to create a file URL for the location file.

Next, add the following methods to DistanceViewController:

```
ARKit/ScavengerHunt/DistanceViewController.swift
private func write(_ location: CLLocation?) {
  guard let location = location else {
    return
  }
  do {
    let data = try NSKeyedArchiver.archivedData(withRootObject: location,
                                                requiringSecureCoding: true)
    try data.write(to: FileManager.locationURL())
  } catch {
    printLog("error: \(error)")
  }
}
```

```
private func loadLocation() -> CLLocation? {
  do {
    let data = try Data(contentsOf: FileManager.locationURL())
    return try NSKeyedUnarchiver.unarchivedObject(
      ofClass: CLLocation.self, from: data)
  } catch {
    printLog("error: \(error)")
  }
  return nil
}
```

This code looks kind of like the code for encoding and decoding objects conforming to Codable. The main difference is that instead of using JSONEncoder and JSONDecoder, we have to use NSKeyedArchiver and NSKeyedUnarchiver, respectively.

You might be wondering why NSKeyedArchiver exists, as we already have JSONEncoder. NSKeyedArchiver is quite an old class, introduced long before Swift even existed. It was the old way to serialize data to disk for later use. On the surface the main difference is that NSKeyedArchiver doesn't store the data in a human-readable format like JSONEncoder does. We use it here because otherwise we would have to introduce a new type and a punch of code to convert from and to CLLocation.

Now let's use these new methods. Replace the storedLocation property with the following code:

ARKit/ScavengerHunt/DistanceViewController.swift
```
private var storedLocation: CLLocation? {
  didSet {
    if let location = storedLocation {
      write(location)
    }
  }
}
```

Here we added a didSet observer to the storedLocation property. The code in the didSet observer is executed each time a new value is assigned to that property. If the assigned value is not nil, we use the write() method to write the location to the documents directory.

We want to load the stored location whenever the distance view appears on-screen. Add the following method to DistanceViewController:

ARKit/ScavengerHunt/DistanceViewController.swift
```
override func viewWillAppear(_ animated: Bool) {
  super.viewWillAppear(animated)

  storedLocation = loadLocation()
}
```

UIKit calls the method viewWillAppear(_:) when the view corresponding to that view controller is going to appear on-screen. This is a good time to load the stored location. Build and run the app on the simulator two times and verify that the location you set on the first run is loaded on the second run. If it doesn't work, make sure you call the methods to write and load the stored location properly.

Adding Virtual Text to Reality

In the beginning of this chapter, we ran the template of an ARKit app on our iPhone. The template let us add alien emojis at the location of the device in the AR view. In the app we're building, we want to add the text to a detected horizontal plane—for example, the ground. In ARKit we can achieve this by adding an instance of ARAnchor to the session of the sceneView.

Adding an Anchor

Anchors can have names, which is useful in apps where you plan to add several different anchors to a scene. In our app we have only one kind of anchor, which means technically we don't need a name for it. Nevertheless, we'll add a name now just to see how it is done.

Open Scene.swift and add the following global constant at the beginning of the file, outside of the Scene class:

ARKit/ScavengerHunt/Scene.swift
```
let textAnchorName = "textAnchorName"
```

Next, change the body of the touchesBegan(_:with:) method such that it looks like following code. The changed lines are highlighted.

ARKit/ScavengerHunt/Scene.swift
```
override func touchesBegan(_ touches: Set<UITouch>, with event: UIEvent?) {
  guard let sceneView = self.view as? ARSKView else {
    return
  }
➤ guard let touch = touches.first else { return }
➤ let point = touch.location(in: sceneView)
➤ guard let hitTestResult =
➤   sceneView.hitTest(point, types: .existingPlane).first else {
➤     return
➤ }
➤
➤ let anchor = ARAnchor(name: textAnchorName,
➤                       transform: hitTestResult.worldTransform)
  sceneView.session.add(anchor: anchor)
}
```

In this code, we check whether the view is an instance of ARSKView. The prefix *ARSK* stands for *Augmented Reality SpriteKit*. Next, we get the location of the first touch in this AR view and check if the touch hit a detected plane in the view. ARKit can detect vertical or horizontal planes in the AR view. If the touch hit a detected plane, we add an anchor to that point.

Before we use this anchor to add some text to the ground, let's present the AR view when the user taps the Add Anchor button.

Presenting the AR View

When the user adds an anchor, we need to present the AR view. Right now the view controller managing the AR view is called ViewController. This is a bad name. Let's change it.

Open ViewController.swift and select the class name. Select the Xcode menu item Editor > Refactor > Rename and change the name to ARViewController.

To be able to instantiate an instance of ARViewController, we need to give it an identifier in the storyboard. Open Main.storyboard, select the ARViewController in the overview, and open the identity inspector with the shortcut ⌥⌘4. Type ARViewController into the Storyboard ID text field.

Pro Tip: Use the Class Name as the StoryboardID

 Use the class name as the StoryboardID. This way you don't need to remember two different names for roughly the same thing. Don't forget to change the name when the class name changes.

Now we can instantiate and present an instance of ARViewController. Add the following method to DistanceViewController:

ARKit/ScavengerHunt/DistanceViewController.swift
```
func showAR() {
  if let next = storyboard?.instantiateViewController(
    withIdentifier: "ARViewController") as? ARViewController {
    next.modalPresentationStyle = .fullScreen
    present(next, animated: true, completion: nil)
  }
}
```

This code instantiates an instance of ARViewController from the storyboard and presents it full-screen to the user. Add the call of this new method at the end of setAnchor(_:):

```
ARKit/ScavengerHunt/DistanceViewController.swift
@IBAction func setAnchor(_ sender: UIButton) {
  storedLocation = locationProvider.lastLocation

➤ showAR()
}
```

Detecting Planes

The changes we made in touchesBegan(_:with:) expect that our ARSession can detect
horizontal planes. It doesn't do that by default because doing so requires a
lot of CPU and drains the battery. But it's very easy to switch on this behavior.
Open ARViewController.swift and add the highlighted line of code in viewWillAppear(_:)
right below the initialization of the ARWorldTrackingConfiguration:

```
ARKit/ScavengerHunt/ARViewController.swift
override func viewWillAppear(_ animated: Bool) {
  super.viewWillAppear(animated)

  // Create a session configuration
  let configuration = ARWorldTrackingConfiguration()
➤ configuration.planeDetection = .horizontal

  // Run the view's session
  sceneView.session.run(configuration)
}
```

Now build and run the app on your iPhone, add an anchor, and move your
iPhone around to scan the floor. Then tap the floor on the screen. With our
changes, the emoji gets added to the floor.

The World Mapping Status

During the scanning process, the user needs to move the device. This is
because ARKit needs to record features on the ground to create a world map.
Depending on the movement of the device, the mapping passes through different mapping stages: limited, extending, and mapped.

Let's add a label that shows the current mapping status in the user interface.
In the exercises you'll change the status to something that is more appropriate
for the user.

Open Main.storyboard and drag a label from the library to the top of the scene
of the ARViewController. Pin it to the top, right, and left edges of the ARSKView using
a padding of 10. Change the alignment to Center and change the background
color to white. When you are done, the result should look like the image on
page 110.

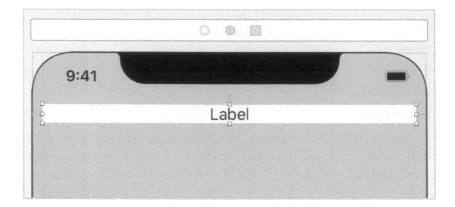

With the label selected, open the assistant editor. Press and hold the `control` key while you drag a connection from the label into ARViewController below the existing outlet. Type in the name statusLabel, select Strong in the last picker, make sure Connection is set to Outlet, and click Connect. Xcode adds the following code:

ARKit/ScavengerHunt/ARViewController.swift
```
@IBOutlet var statusLabel: UILabel!
```

The ARSession informs its delegate about the mapping status. The delegate needs to conform to the ARSessionDelegate protocol, so we add that protocol to ARViewController.

ARKit/ScavengerHunt/ARViewController.swift
```
class ARViewController: UIViewController,
  ARSKViewDelegate, ARSessionDelegate {
```

Now we can set the delegate of the AR session. Add the highlighted code in viewDidLoad():

ARKit/ScavengerHunt/ARViewController.swift
```
override func viewDidLoad() {
  super.viewDidLoad()

  // Set the view's delegate
  sceneView.delegate = self
  sceneView.session.delegate = self

  // Show statistics such as fps and node count
  sceneView.showsFPS = true
  sceneView.showsNodeCount = true

  // Load the SKScene from 'Scene.sks'
  if let scene = SKScene(fileNamed: "Scene") {
    sceneView.presentScene(scene)
  }
}
```

Then add the following delegate method to ARViewController:

ARKit/ScavengerHunt/ARViewController.swift
```swift
func session(_ session: ARSession, didUpdate frame: ARFrame) {

  switch frame.worldMappingStatus {
  case .limited:
    statusLabel.text = "Limited"
  case .extending:
    statusLabel.text = "Extending"
  case .mapped:
    statusLabel.text = "Mapped"
  default:
    statusLabel.text = "Not available"
  }
}
```

In this method, we just set the status to the status label. Build and run the app on your iPhone, select the Set Anchor tab, and scan a horizontal plane. Verify that the status label updates when the status changes.

Place Some Virtual Text

Now let's change the code that adds the label node to the ARSKView. We want to add some text to the AR view. Replace the method view(_:nodeFor:) with the following code:

ARKit/ScavengerHunt/ARViewController.swift
```swift
func view(_ view: ARSKView, nodeFor anchor: ARAnchor) -> SKNode? {

  if anchor.name == textAnchorName {
    let labelNode = SKLabelNode(text: "Hi!")
    labelNode.fontName = "AvenirNext-Bold"
    labelNode.fontSize = 50
    labelNode.fontColor = .red
    labelNode.horizontalAlignmentMode = .center
    labelNode.verticalAlignmentMode = .center

    for i in 5...15 {
      let circleNode = SKShapeNode(circleOfRadius: CGFloat(20*i))
      circleNode.strokeColor = .yellow
      labelNode.addChild(circleNode)
    }
    return labelNode
  } else {
    return nil
  }
}
```

We added the if clause to check the name of the anchor. As mentioned before, this check isn't needed here because we have only one type of anchor. I added it in this example to show you how it can be done. In addition, we changed the font to AvenirNext-Bold and changed the size and the font color. In the for loop, we add circles to make the text easier to find. Build and run the app on your iPhone and verify that you can now add text to a horizontal plane.

It works! Now we can draw text on the ground using ARKit. In the next section we'll store the world map to the file system to reload it later.

Storing the World Map

As of iOS 12, we can get the world map the user has assembled and store it for later use. For that to work, we need somewhere to store the world map. Open FileManagerExtension and add the following method:

ARKit/ScavengerHunt/FileManagerExtension.swift
```
static func mapDataURL() -> URL {
  return documentsURL().appendingPathComponent("mapData")
}
```

Next, we need to add a button to the user interface that triggers storing the world map. Open Main.storyboard and drag a button to the lower-right corner of the ARSKView. Pin the button to the bottom and left edge of the super view with a margin of 10 points.

Open the attribute inspector, change the title of the button to Done, and set the background color to white.

The button looks a bit strange right now—there's no padding around its title. Open the size inspector with the shortcut ⌥⌘6 and change the content inset of the button such that the user interface looks like the following image. I used an inset of 10 points for left and right and an inset of 5 for top and bottom.

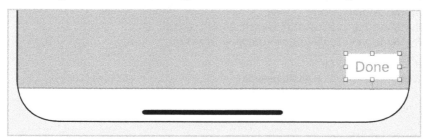

Open the assistant editor. Press and hold the control and drag a connection from the button to right above the closing curly braces of ARViewController. Type in the name done, change the type to UIButton, and click Connect.

Open ARViewController.swift and import the LogStore logging library below the existing import statements:

ARKit/ScavengerHunt/ARViewController.swift

```swift
import UIKit
import SpriteKit
import ARKit
import LogStore
```

Then change the done(_:) method so that it looks like this:

ARKit/ScavengerHunt/ARViewController.swift

```swift
@IBAction func done(_ sender: UIButton) {
  sceneView.session.getCurrentWorldMap { [weak self] worldMap, error in

    guard let worldMap = worldMap else {
      // ToDo: Present an alert about the error.
      printLog("error: \(String(describing: error))")
      return
    }

    do {
      let data =
        try NSKeyedArchiver.archivedData(withRootObject: worldMap,
                                         requiringSecureCoding: false)
      try data.write(to: FileManager.mapDataURL())
      self?.dismiss(animated: true, completion: nil)
    } catch {
      printLog("error: \(error)")
    }
  }
}
```

To get the world map, we call the method getCurrentWorldMap(completionHandler:) on the instance of ARSession. Generating the world map can take some time. When it's ready, the completion handler (the closure we provide in the method call) is called.

We check if the world map is not nil. In this case we generate an instance of Data using NSKeyedArchiver. This is possible because ARWorldMap conforms to the protocol NSSecureCoding. When the data object is generated, we write it to the documents directory and dismiss the AR view controller.

Our app works best when we make sure the world mapping state is mapped before we get the current world map. Let's disable the Done button as long as the mapping state is not mapped.

Open Main.storyboard, select the ARViewConroller in the overview, and activate the assistant editor if it's not still open. Press and hold the control key and drag a connection from the Done button to right below the existing properties. Type in the name doneButton and click Connect. Xcode adds the following code:

```
ARKit/ScavengerHunt/ARViewController.swift
@IBOutlet var doneButton: UIButton!
```

Next add the highlighted line to the body of session(_:didUpdate:):

```
ARKit/ScavengerHunt/ARViewController.swift
func session(_ session: ARSession, didUpdate frame: ARFrame) {

  doneButton.isEnabled = frame.worldMappingStatus == .mapped

  switch frame.worldMappingStatus {
  case .limited:
    statusLabel.text = "Limited"
  case .extending:
    statusLabel.text = "Extending"
  case .mapped:
    statusLabel.text = "Mapped"
  default:
    statusLabel.text = "Not available"
  }
}
```

When this method gets called by the augmented reality session, we enable the button only if the mapping status is mapped. Build and run the app on your iPhone and verify that the Done button works as expected. If it doesn't work, confirm that the button is connected to the code and that creating the world map doesn't result in an error.

In the next section, we'll display the AR view when the user approaches the stored location.

Presenting the Augmented Reality View

When the user taps the Done button, the AR view is dismissed and the distance view is shown again. Then the user should walk to another place and pass the iPhone to another player. This player can then use the distance information to find the text location. In this section, we'll program our app to show the stored world map when the user is within 10 meters of the stored location and can start searching the ground for the text using the AR view.

We already have a method that presents the AR view to the user. But we need to tell the ARViewController instance whether it should load the stored world map. Add the following property to ARViewController:

```
ARKit/ScavengerHunt/ARViewController.swift
var shouldRestore = false
```

We'll use this property later to decide whether we should load a stored world map or start with a new one.

Now open DistanceViewController.swift and change showAR() so that it looks like the following code. The lines that have changed are highlighted.

ARKit/ScavengerHunt/DistanceViewController.swift

```
➤   func showAR(shouldRestore: Bool = false) {

      if let next = storyboard?.instantiateViewController(
        withIdentifier: "ARViewController") as? ARViewController {

➤       next.shouldRestore = shouldRestore
        next.modalPresentationStyle = .fullScreen
        present(next, animated: true, completion: nil)
      }
    }
  }
```

We added the optional parameter shouldRestore. The value of this parameter is passed to the instance of ARViewController.

When the distance to the stored location is less than 10 meters, we want to present the AR view. Add the highlighted code in updateUI(for:) right after the code lastDistance = distance:

ARKit/ScavengerHunt/DistanceViewController.swift

```
  func updateUI(for location: CLLocation?) {

    guard let location = location else {
      return
    }

    if let storedLocation = storedLocation {

      let distance = location.distance(from: storedLocation)
      distanceLabel.text = String(format: "%.2lf m", distance)

      if lastDistance < distance {
        view.backgroundColor = .red
      } else if lastDistance > distance {
        view.backgroundColor = .green
      }

      lastDistance = distance

➤     if distance < 10 {
➤       showAR(shouldRestore: true)
➤     }
    } else {
      let coordinate = location.coordinate
      distanceLabel.text = String(format: "%.6lf, %.6lf",
                                  coordinate.latitude,
                                  coordinate.longitude)
    }
  }
```

Make sure that the latitude of the custom location is set to 1.0001 and the longitude is set to 2. Then build and run the app on the simulator. The app should show the distance view with a distance of 11.06 m. Next, change the latitude to 1. Our app shows the AR view.

This works—nice. But there's a problem with this implementation. When the user taps the Done button, the AR view is dismissed. But since the user is still within 10 meters of the stored location, the AR view is immediately presented again.

Let's add some code to ensure that the AR view won't be shown again until the user leaves the 10-meter radius. Add the following property to DistanceViewController:

ARKit/ScavengerHunt/DistanceViewController.swift
```swift
private var stillInRadius = false
```

When the AR view is presented to the user, we set this property to true. Add the highlighted line at the beginning of showAR(shouldRestore:):

ARKit/ScavengerHunt/DistanceViewController.swift
```swift
func showAR(shouldRestore: Bool = false) {

    stillInRadius = true

    if let next = storyboard?.instantiateViewController(
        withIdentifier: "ARViewController") as? ARViewController {

        next.shouldRestore = shouldRestore
        next.modalPresentationStyle = .fullScreen
        present(next, animated: true, completion: nil)
    }
}
```

Replace the code we added to updateUI(for:) to present the AR view with the following code. The changed lines are highlighted.

ARKit/ScavengerHunt/DistanceViewController.swift
```swift
func updateUI(for location: CLLocation?) {

    guard let location = location else {
        return
    }

    if let storedLocation = storedLocation {

        let distance = location.distance(from: storedLocation)
        distanceLabel.text = String(format: "%.2lf m", distance)

        if lastDistance < distance {
            view.backgroundColor = .red
        } else if lastDistance > distance {
            view.backgroundColor = .green
        }

        lastDistance = distance
```

```swift
      if distance < 10 {
➤       if stillInRadius == false {
          showAR(shouldRestore: true)
➤       }
➤     } else {
➤       stillInRadius = false
      }
    } else {
      let coordinate = location.coordinate
      distanceLabel.text = String(format: "%.6lf, %.6lf",
                                  coordinate.latitude,
                                  coordinate.longitude)
  }
}
```

In this code we check if the property stillInRadius is false. Only then do we present the AR view when the user is within 10 meters of the stored location. We also set the property to false when the user is outside of the 10-meter radius. This should do the trick. In the next section we'll load the stored world map from the documents directory.

Restoring the World Map

The last thing we need to do to make the first version of our little app work is to load the world map. We already added a property to ARViewController to control when the world map should be loaded. Add the highlighted code to viewWillAppear(_:) right above the line where we set the session delegate:

```swift
ARKit/ScavengerHunt/ARViewController.swift
override func viewWillAppear(_ animated: Bool) {
  super.viewWillAppear(animated)

  // Create a session configuration
  let configuration = ARWorldTrackingConfiguration()
  configuration.planeDetection = .horizontal

➤ if shouldRestore {
➤   do {
➤     let data = try Data(contentsOf: FileManager.mapDataURL())
➤     let worldMap = try NSKeyedUnarchiver.unarchivedObject(
➤       ofClass: ARWorldMap.self, from: data)
➤     configuration.initialWorldMap = worldMap
➤   } catch {
➤     printLog("error: \(error)")
➤   }
➤ }

  // Run the view's session
  sceneView.session.run(configuration)
}
```

When shouldRestore is set to true, we load the world map data from the documents directory and try to unpack it from the archive. If this is successful, we set the loaded world map to the initialWorldMap property of the world tracking configuration. This is all we have to do to reload a stored world map—it could hardly be simpler.

Build and run the app on your iPhone and try it out. Add an anchor, add some text, and verify that the world map with the text is loaded when you leave and reenter the 10-meter radius around the stored location.

You might have noticed that the accuracy of the stored location is sometimes not that good. You'll improve that in the exercises.

That's it! The first version of our Scavenger Hunt app is finished. Don't forget to work through the exercises to improve on this initial version.

Exercises

1. The accuracy of the location from the iPhone improves over time. The reason for this is that it needs some time for the GPS sensor to receive information from the GPS satellites. Add a label to the DistanceViewController that shows the accuracy as long as no location is stored. The accuracy is delivered in the CLLocation instance.

2. Add a label or an alert that informs the users that they have to leave and reenter the 10-meter radius after they have set the anchor.

3. Let the user type in the text that is drawn on the ground.

4. Change the world mapping status text shown to the user. Make it meaningful for the user.

Debugging on the Go

A good log often tells the story of a bug. What happened right before the bug appeared? What did the user expect to happen instead? Which classes are involved in the problematic part of the app?

In this appendix we'll build a library that will allow you to check the log output within a running app. It's important to make this library small and encapsulated so that you can use it in all your apps from now on. The apps we've built throughout this book are all apps that need to be tested outside. Seeing the log while you're away from your Mac and Xcode will be very useful.

Creating a Host Application

We're going to build our logging library step by step, but to verify that each step brings us closer to our goal, we first need something to log. We'll build a simple demo app that acts as a host app for developing the library.

Open Xcode and create a new project by selecting the menu item File > New > Project.... Select the iOS > Single View App template and click Next. Type LogStoreDevelopment for the Product Name. For the user interface, select Storyboard from the drop-down menu and deselect the check marks for Use Core Data, Include Unit Tests, and Include UI Tests, as shown in the image on page 120. Click Next and select a place to store the project. Then click Create.

Now that we have a host app to test our library, we can work on the library itself.

Let's create a Swift package for it, because this is the preferred way to share code between projects.

Creating a Swift Package

Creating a Swift package is quite easy. In Xcode, select the menu item File >
New > Swift Package.... Xcode presents a pop-up window for the initial settings
of the package. Type LogStore in the Save As field. At the bottom of the window
are two drop-down menus, "Add to" and "Group," as shown in the following
image. Select LogStoreDevelopment from the "Add to" menu to add the package
to the project and then select LogStoreDevelopment again from the "Group" menu
to add it to the root folder.

With these settings, we've added the newly created package to the project we're currently working on. Click Create. Xcode reloads and shows you the created package.

Let's have a look at what's in there. First, you'll see a file named Package.swift. This is the manifest, which comprises all information needed to build the package. For example, if our package depends on other packages, that information would go here.

As Swift packages are the Swift way to share code between different projects, Xcode creates a README file for you. For decades, README files have been the standard way to let developers know what a library does. Let's follow this tradition and add a sentence about what this package will do. Click README.md to open it in the Xcode editor. Replace the template text with this:

A tiny package to make log output accessible from within an iOS app.

Make a mental note that we have to update this file once we know how the package is used.

Pro Tip: Always Add a Package Description

 You should always take a few minutes to add information about the package. Your future self will thank you. And don't forget to update the information as the package evolves.

At the moment, the host app has no idea there's a library it can use. Even though the package is in the project of the host app, we have to add the resulting library to its *target* in a separate step. Targets are what Xcode uses to manage build products. For example, if you created an app with a Watch app companion, you'd have two or more targets in the same project. Our host app has only one target. Let's add the library generated by the Swift package to this target.

Open the project navigator and select the topmost element with the blue icon, LogStoreDevelopment. Xcode opens the project settings. To open the target settings, select the target in the TARGETS overview. Make sure the General tab is selected. Scroll down until you see the section Frameworks, Libraries, and Embedded Content. Click the + button to add a new library. In the pop-up window, select the LogStore library and click Add.

The image on page 122 shows what you should see on your screen.

Done! We can now use the package in the host app. Our Swift package is set up, so now let's fill it with life.

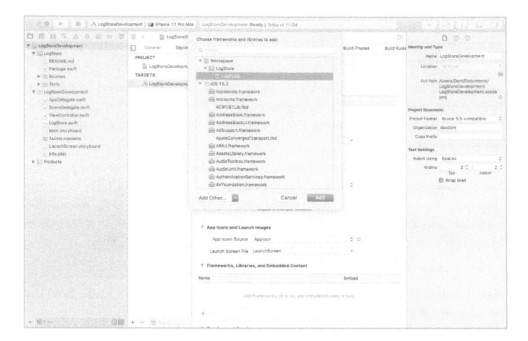

The library we want to build needs to do two things: first, it needs to store the log somewhere, and second, it needs to provide a way to access the log and display the content within the app. Let's start with the easy part: storing the log.

Creating the LogStore

The LogStore will store the log in an array of strings. During package creation, Xcode added a Sources folder for the code. That folder contains a subfolder with one source code file, LogStore.swift. Replace the contents of that file with the following code:

Debugging/LogStoreDevelopment/LogStore/Sources/LogStore/LogStore.swift

```
import Foundation

struct LogStore {
  static var log: [String] = []
}
```

Note the keyword static. Properties with this keyword are stored in the type itself. Such properties are called *type properties*. This means we don't need to create an instance of LogStore to access the log array. Instead, we can access it with LogStore.log.

Usually we print log output using the global print() function. We want a similar function that prints to the debug console and also adds the string to the log array. This means the function needs to be defined in the global scope and not within the LogStore or any other type. Add the printLog() function to Log-Store.swift as shown in the following code. The added lines are highlighted.

```
Debugging/LogStoreDevelopment/LogStore/Sources/LogStore/LogStore.swift
import Foundation

struct LogStore {
  static var log: [String] = []
}

➤ public func printLog(_ string: String) {
➤   print(string)
➤
➤   LogStore.log.append(string)
➤ }
```

This is all we need to store the log for later access from within the app. With this, the first part of our little library is finished and we can move on to the second part—presenting the log in the host app.

Presenting the Log On-Screen

Our library can store log entries, but this alone is not really useful. We need a component that will display the log entries on-screen so that when our app isn't working properly we can figure out why.

The log itself is just an array with short strings, so a UITableView is the perfect component to display that data. Whenever you see information in similar chunks in an app (for example, tweets or Facebook posts), a table view is probably presenting that information. The easiest way to get a table view to display on-screen is to use a table view controller.

Let's add a UITableViewController to the libraries package.

Select the LogStore folder in the package, add a new file with the shortcut ⌘N, and change the file name to LogViewController.swift. Xcode creates a file with just one statement: import Foundation. The class UITableViewController is defined in UIKit, like all the user interface components in iOS development. Replace import Foundation with import UIKit.

Next, add the minimal code needed to define a table view controller:

```
Debugging/LogStoreDevelopment/LogStore/Sources/LogStore/LogViewController.swift
import UIKit

public class LogViewController : UITableViewController {
}
```

The keyword public tells Xcode that this class should be accessible from other modules. We need this here because we want to create an instance of this class in the app target to test if the package is set up correctly.

Before we can use the library in the host app, we need to import it. Open ViewController.swift in the Xcode editor and import LogStore right below the existing import statement.

```
Debugging/LogStoreDevelopment/LogStoreDevelopment/ViewController.swift
import UIKit
import LogStore
```

Add the following method within the ViewController class:

```
Debugging/LogStoreDevelopment/LogStoreDevelopment/ViewController.swift
override func viewDidAppear(_ animated: Bool) {
  super.viewDidAppear(animated)

  let logViewController = LogViewController()
  present(logViewController, animated: true)
}
```

With this code, we create an instance of LogViewController and present it modally on the initial view controller. This code is located in viewDidAppear(_:) because the view of the initial view controller needs to appear on-screen before we can present another view controller on top of it. Xcode might show an error that it can't find LogViewController. This is because we still have to compile the project to make our host app aware of the changes we just introduced into the package.

Pro Tip: Watch the Debug Output

When running your app on a simulator or on your device, always keep an eye on the output of the debug console. Xcode often gives you hints about what's wrong if something doesn't work as expected. Try to understand what Xcode prints to the log. The better you are at understanding the console output, the easier it is to find and fix errors.

Although Xcode often tells you exactly what's going on or what needs to be improved, sometimes you still won't understand what's wrong or what you need to do. In these cases, you can search for answers on the Internet using keywords from the console output. Someone else has probably had the same problem and gotten answers on sites like StackOverflow.com.

Build and run the app on your favorite iOS simulator. After the app has loaded, you'll see an empty table view on-screen. This means we can access classes that are defined in the package from outside of the package.

Currently, the LogViewController just shows an empty table view. This is the default implementation of UITableViewController. To show the log strings, we first need to register a table view cell. Open LogViewController.swift and add the following code:

Debugging/LogStoreDevelopment/LogStore/Sources/LogStore/LogViewController.swift

```
public override func viewDidLoad() {
  super.viewDidLoad()

  tableView.register(UITableViewCell.self,
                    forCellReuseIdentifier: "Cell")
}
```

When a view of a view controller has completely loaded, UIKit calls the view controller method viewDidLoad(). In a table view controller, this is the perfect time to register a cell. We register the cell class UITableViewCell by calling register(_:forCellReuseIdentifier:) on the table view. As the information we want to show in this table view consists only of short text strings, a plain UITableViewCell is enough.

Joe asks:
Why Do We Need to Register a Cell?

UIKit usually registers the cell when the storyboard is loaded. You just have to drag the table view cell into a scene of the storyboard, and the rest is done for you at runtime.

At the time of writing, Swift packages do not support resources. This means we can't add a storyboard to the package and have to do all the setup in code. Fortunately, as you'll see shortly, this is quite easy.

Now that the table view cell is registered, let's use it to show log entries. Add the highlighted property at the beginning of the class LogViewController.

Debugging/LogStoreDevelopment/LogStore/Sources/LogStore/LogViewController.swift

```
public class LogViewController : UITableViewController {

➤   let logItems = LogStore.log

    public override func viewDidLoad() {
      super.viewDidLoad()

      tableView.register(UITableViewCell.self,
                        forCellReuseIdentifier: "Cell")
    }
}
```

Here we assign the log array in the LogStore type to a property of the table view controller. We could have used the LogStore.log directly, but using a property makes the code easier to read.

Pro Tip: Always Optimize Your Code for Reading

Code is written once but read many times, so it should be easy to read and understand.

One important characteristic of readable code is a good name. In this example, logItems is easier to understand than LogStore.log. We could even take this a bit further and change the name of the property in LogStore to logItems as well.

Think about that yourself. Which name would you choose for the property?

There's much more you can do to make code readable, but writing readable code is beyond the scope of this book. However, there are many books out there on that topic. For example, see *The Art of Readable Code [BF12]* or *Code Complete [McC04]*.

The table view should show as many cells as there are log elements in the log array. To achieve that, add the following method below the viewDidLoad() method:

Debugging/LogStoreDevelopment/LogStore/Sources/LogStore/LogViewController.swift
```swift
public override func tableView(_ tableView: UITableView,
                                 numberOfRowsInSection section: Int)
  -> Int {
    return logItems.count
}
```

Now we're ready to fill and return the cell. Add the following method at the end of LogViewController:

Debugging/LogStoreDevelopment/LogStore/Sources/LogStore/LogViewController.swift
```swift
public override func tableView(_ tableView: UITableView,
                                 cellForRowAt indexPath: IndexPath)
  -> UITableViewCell {
    let cell = tableView.dequeueReusableCell(withIdentifier: "Cell",
                                               for: indexPath)
    cell.textLabel?.text = logItems[indexPath.row]
    return cell
}
```

To improve scroll performance and reduce memory usage, table views put cells that are no longer visible on-screen into a reuse pool. By calling dequeueReusableCell(withIdentifier:for:), we ask the table view to dequeue a suitable cell for that identifier from that pool. This technique works only when a cell for that identifier was registered in a storyboard or in code. If there's no cell available for dequeuing, the table view creates a new one. Next, we assign the log entry for that row to the text property of the text label in the cell.

Let's log something and see if the log store works. To add a log entry when the app starts, open ViewController.swift and add the highlighted line in the following code to viewDidLoad():

```
Debugging/LogStoreDevelopment/LogStoreDevelopment/ViewController.swift
override func viewDidLoad() {
  super.viewDidLoad()

➤  printLog("viewDidLoad")
}
```

Build and run the app on the simulator. It works!

If you don't see the table with the log output, as in the following image, make sure you're using printLog() instead of print(). If the app still doesn't work, retrace the steps you just did and compare them with your code.

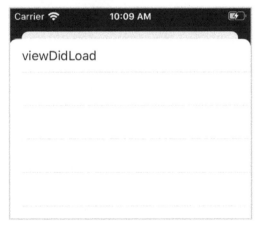

Next, we need to find a way to present the log to users when they perform a special gesture with the device.

Presenting the Log from a Special Shake

We could add a button to the user interface to trigger the presentation of the log entries, but this isn't practical because we'd have to add it to each view controller in the app. It's more elegant to present the log when the iPhone registers a special gesture.

iPhones are packed with sensors. In Chapter 2, Measuring Length with Gravitation, on page 33, we used the accelerometer to measure the length of a swing. In this appendix, we use it to react to the action of knocking the left side of your phone against your left palm, as shown in the following image.

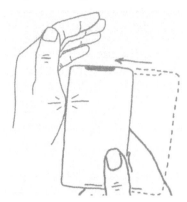

This gesture results in a rapid deceleration. The accelerometer in the iPhone can measure acceleration and deceleration.

Whenever this gesture is detected, the library should present the log. The easiest way to make the app react to this gesture is to create a class that listens to motion events.

Creating a Log Trigger

Select the LogStore folder in the LogStore library and press ⌘N. Rename the added file to LogTrigger.swift. The log trigger needs to hold a reference to the key window to be able to figure out how to display the view controller with the log entries on-screen. The key window of the app is an instance of UIWindow, which is defined in UIKit. Replace import Foundation with import UIKit.

iOS delivers motion data from the sensors to an instance of CMMotionManager, which is defined in the CoreMotion framework. Insert import CoreMotion right below the existing import statement and add the following class definition to LogTrigger.swift:

Debugging/LogStoreDevelopment/LogStore/Sources/LogStore/LogTrigger.swift
```swift
import UIKit
import CoreMotion

public class LogTrigger {

  let window: UIWindow?
  let motionManager = CMMotionManager()

  public init(in window: UIWindow?) {

    self.window = window

  }
}
```

With this code, we define a class with two properties, one of type UIWindow and one of type CMMotionManager. The window is passed into this class through the initializer.

Next, we have to activate the delivery of motion events. Add the highlighted lines in the following code to LogTrigger:

Debugging/LogStoreDevelopment/LogStore/Sources/LogStore/LogTrigger.swift

```
public init(in window: UIWindow?) {

    self.window = window

➤   motionManager.startAccelerometerUpdates(to: .main) {
➤     [weak self] data, error in
➤
➤     guard let data = data else { return }
➤     if data.acceleration.x < -5 {
➤       printLog("x acceleration: \(data.acceleration.x)")
➤       self?.presentLog()
➤     }
➤   }
  }

➤ func presentLog() {
➤ }
```

To activate the delivery of motion events, we call startAccelerometerUpdates(to:with-Handler:). Whenever there's a new accelerometer event, the code between the curly braces is executed. This structure is called a *closure*.

In the closure, we use a guard let statement to unwrap the data parameter because it's an optional. This means the value of the parameter could be either nil or an instance of Data. If the value is nil, the code between the curly braces after the else keyword is executed. If the value is not nil, data contains the unwrapped Data instance and the code below the guard let statement is executed. We use the unwrapped data object to check if the acceleration in the x direction is less than –5. This means the body of the if clause is executed when the device is quickly stopped after moving to the left. (I came up with the number –5 after doing some experiments with the accelerometer.)

Next, we need to activate our log trigger. Open SceneDelegate.swift and import LogStore below the existing import statement:

Debugging/LogStoreDevelopment/LogStoreDevelopment/SceneDelegate.swift

```
import UIKit
import LogStore
```

Build the project with the shortcut ⌘B to make the LogStore package available in the main target. Add the highlighted lines in the following code to SceneDelegate:

Debugging/LogStoreDevelopment/LogStoreDevelopment/SceneDelegate.swift
```swift
class SceneDelegate: UIResponder, UIWindowSceneDelegate {

  var window: UIWindow?
➤ var trigger: LogTrigger?

  func scene(_ scene: UIScene,
             willConnectTo session: UISceneSession,
             options connectionOptions: UIScene.ConnectionOptions) {

    guard let _ = (scene as? UIWindowScene) else { return }

➤   trigger = LogTrigger(in: window)
  }
  // ...
  // other methods
  // ...

}
```

With these changes, we add a property for the log trigger and initialize it in scene(_:willConnectTo:options:) with the window property. This is all we have to do to set up the motion trigger.

Connect your iPhone and build and run the application on it. After the app has fully loaded, the log is presented as before. But now when you perform the trigger gesture, the acceleration in the x direction is printed to the debug console.

Wow, this is cool! Let's look at what we've just done. We've created and activated a class that can trigger actions when the iPhone is moved in a certain way. This opens up many interesting opportunities to experiment with useful little development tools like the one we're currently building.

Now we want to present the log to the users when they perform the special shake of the device. But first, delete the whole method viewDidAppear(animated:) from ViewController as we don't need it anymore.

Presenting the Log

In iOS, views are stacked on top of each other. The stack is called the *view hierarchy*. We can present a new view controller only on top of the one corresponding to the visible view. This means that to present the log to the user, we first need to figure out the topmost view and its view controller. Add the following method to LogTrigger:

Debugging/LogStoreDevelopment/LogStore/Sources/LogStore/LogTrigger.swift
```swift
func visibleViewController(
  from viewController: UIViewController?) -> UIViewController? {
```

```
  if let navigationController =
    viewController as? UINavigationController {

    return visibleViewController(
      from: navigationController.topViewController)
  }
  if let tabBarController =
    viewController as? UITabBarController {

    return visibleViewController(
      from: tabBarController.selectedViewController)
  }
  if let presentedViewController =
    viewController?.presentedViewController {

    return visibleViewController(
      from: presentedViewController)
  }

  return viewController
}
```

This code looks a bit complicated, so let's go through it step by step. First, we check if the passed-in view controller is an instance of UINavigationController. A UINavigationController manages several view controllers in a *navigation stack*. The topmost view controller can be accessed through the topViewController property. Because the topViewController itself could present another view controller modally, we need to call visibleViewController(from:) again.

If the passed-in view controller is an instance of UITabBarController, we call the method again with the selectedViewController because this is the view controller for the selected tab. If presentedViewController of the passed-in view controller is set, we call the method again with this. If neither case applies, we're finished and have found the visible view controller.

Using these steps, we walk the view hierarchy from bottom to top to the view controller of the visible view. The only step left is to select an entry point, which is quite easy to do. We can use the rootViewController of the trigger window, as this is at the root of the view hierarchy.

To put that all together, replace presentLog() with the following code:

Debugging/LogStoreDevelopment/LogStore/Sources/LogStore/LogTrigger.swift
```
func presentLog() {
  let visible = visibleViewController(from: window?.rootViewController)
  let logViewController = LogViewController()
  visible?.present(logViewController, animated: true)
}
```

With this code, we get the visible view controller and display an instance of LogViewController on top of it. And finally, we're done! Build and run the app and perform the gesture to make sure that everything works as expected.

Your first version of a simple logging library is finished. In the exercises you'll improve it with easy additions.

Loading the package to a hosted service like GitHub, GitLab, or Bitbucket will make it easily reusable in other projects. The next section explains how to do this.

Sharing the Package on GitHub

The easiest way to include your new package in all the projects you're working on is to load it to a service like GitHub, GitLab, or Bitbucket. In this section we'll use GitHub, but the other services work in a similar fashion. To follow along you'll need an account for one of those services, if you don't already have one.

First, we need to move the package out of the project directory. Press and hold the option key and drag the package from Xcode to somewhere in the file system on your Mac. macOS creates a copy of the package at the drag destination. In Xcode, use the shortcut ⌘O to open the directory of the package. Alternatively, you can open the manifest in Xcode to open the package in Xcode.

To put the package under source control, select the Source Control > Create Git Repositories... menu item. In the window that appears, click the Create button. Xcode adds a Git repository to the project. To add all the package files to that repository, select Source Control > Commit. Check the box next to all the files and folders in the package, add the commit message "Initial commit", and click the button Commit 6 Files.

To load the package to GitHub, we need to log in from within Xcode. Open Xcode preferences and add your GitHub (or GitLab or Bitbucket) account.

Now open the source control navigator with the shortcut ⌘2. Press and hold the control key and click the repository in the source control navigator. In the pop-up menu that appears, select Create "LogStore" Remote. In the next window you can decide how the repository should be hosted on GitHub. Check the settings, change them if needed, and then click Create.

The Swift Package Manager needs tags in the repository to work properly. Again, press and hold the control key and click the repository. In the pop-up menu that appears, select Tag "master".... Type in the tag 1.0.0 and click Create.

Finally we can push the packages to GitHub. Select the Source Control > Push... menu item. Select the "Include tags" check box and click Push.

The package is now on GitHub, and you can use it in all your projects from now on.

Wrapping Up

We covered a lot in this appendix. We wrote a small library that displays the login response of motion events delivered by the device. To make that library easy to add to all our projects, we put that code into its own Swift package and loaded the package to a hosted source control service. We did all of this without the use of storyboards, as Swift packages don't support resources at the moment.

Exercises

Here are some exercises to apply what you've learned and to make the library more useful:

1. If the text of a log entry doesn't fit on one line, the text is truncated. Change the code in tableView(_:cellForRowAt:) to allow wrapping of longer log entries.

2. To make the log look more like the debug output in Xcode, remove the cell separators.

3. Add the time to the log entries.

4. Make LogStore conform to the protocol Codable and write the log to a file when the app is closed.

5. Sometimes it's useful to have the log on your Mac for further investigation. Add the feature to send the log via email.

Bibliography

[BF12]   Dustin Boswell and Trevor Foucher. *The Art of Readable Code*. O'Reilly
          Media, Inc., Sebastopol, CA, 2012.

[McC04]   Steve McConnell. *Code Complete: A Practical Handbook of Software Con-*
          struction, Second Edition. Microsoft Press, Redmond, WA, 2004.

Thank you!

How did you enjoy this book? Please let us know. Take a moment and email us at support@pragprog.com with your feedback. Tell us your story and you could win free ebooks. Please use the subject line "Book Feedback."

Ready for your next great Pragmatic Bookshelf book? Come on over to https://pragprog.com and use the coupon code BUYANOTHER2020 to save 30% on your next ebook.

Void where prohibited, restricted, or otherwise unwelcome. Do not use ebooks near water. If rash persists, see a doctor. Doesn't apply to *The Pragmatic Programmer* ebook because it's older than the Pragmatic Bookshelf itself. Side effects may include increased knowledge and skill, increased marketability, and deep satisfaction. Increase dosage regularly.

And thank you for your continued support,

Andy Hunt, Publisher

SAVE 30%!
Use coupon code
BUYANOTHER2020

iOS Unit Testing by Example

Fearlessly change the design of your iOS code with solid unit tests. Use Xcode's built-in test framework XCTest and Swift to get rapid feedback on all your code — including legacy code. Learn the tricks and techniques of testing all iOS code, especially view controllers (UIViewControllers), which are critical to iOS apps. Learn to isolate and replace dependencies in legacy code written without tests. Practice safe refactoring that makes these tests possible, and watch all your changes get verified quickly and automatically. Make even the boldest code changes with complete confidence.

Jon Reid
(358 pages) ISBN: 9781680506815. $47.95
https://pragprog.com/book/jrlegios

Become an Effective Software Engineering Manager

Software startups make global headlines every day. As technology companies succeed and grow, so do their engineering departments. In your career, you'll may suddenly get the opportunity to lead teams: to become a manager. But this is often uncharted territory. How do you decide whether this career move is right for you? And if you do, what do you need to learn to succeed? Where do you start? How do you know that you're doing it right? What does "it" even mean? And isn't management a dirty word? This book will share the secrets you need to know to manage engineers successfully.

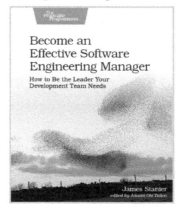

James Stanier
(396 pages) ISBN: 9781680507249. $45.95
https://pragprog.com/book/jsengman

Build Websites with Hugo

Rediscover how fun web development can be with Hugo, the static site generator and web framework that lets you build content sites quickly, using the skills you already have. Design layouts with HTML and share common components across pages. Create Markdown templates that let you create new content quickly. Consume and generate JSON, enhance layouts with logic, and generate a site that works on any platform with no runtime dependencies or database. Hugo gives you everything you need to build your next content site and have fun doing it.

Brian P. Hogan
(154 pages) ISBN: 9781680507263. $26.95
https://pragprog.com/book/bhhugo

Practical Microservices

MVC and CRUD make software easier to write, but harder to change. Microservice-based architectures can help even the smallest of projects remain agile in the long term, but most tutorials meander in theory or completely miss the point of what it means to be microservice based. Roll up your sleeves with real projects and learn the most important concepts of evented architectures. You'll have your own deployable, testable project and a direction for where to go next.

Ethan Garofolo
(290 pages) ISBN: 9781680506457. $45.95
https://pragprog.com/book/egmicro

Real-Time Phoenix

Give users the real-time experience they expect, by using Elixir and Phoenix Channels to build applications that instantly react to changes and reflect the application's true state. Learn how Elixir and Phoenix make it easy and enjoyable to create real-time applications that scale to a large number of users. Apply system design and development best practices to create applications that are easy to maintain. Gain confidence by learning how to break your applications before your users do. Deploy applications with minimized resource use and maximized performance.

Stephen Bussey
(326 pages) ISBN: 9781680507195. $45.95
https://pragprog.com/book/sbsockets

Programming Machine Learning

You've decided to tackle machine learning — because you're job hunting, embarking on a new project, or just think self-driving cars are cool. But where to start? It's easy to be intimidated, even as a software developer. The good news is that it doesn't have to be that hard. Master machine learning by writing code one line at a time, from simple learning programs all the way to a true deep learning system. Tackle the hard topics by breaking them down so they're easier to understand, and build your confidence by getting your hands dirty.

Paolo Perrotta
(340 pages) ISBN: 9781680506600. $47.95
https://pragprog.com/book/pplearn

Competing with Unicorns

Today's tech unicorns develop software differently. They've developed a way of working that lets them scale like an enterprise while working like a startup. These techniques can be learned. This book takes you behind the scenes and shows you how companies like Google, Facebook, and Spotify do it. Leverage their insights, so your teams can work better together, ship higher-quality product faster, innovate more quickly, and compete with the unicorns.

Jonathan Rasmusson
(138 pages) ISBN: 9781680507232. $26.95
https://pragprog.com/book/jragile

Programming Flutter

Develop your next app with Flutter and deliver native look, feel, and performance on both iOS and Android from a single code base. Bring along your favorite libraries and existing code from Java, Kotlin, Objective-C, and Swift, so you don't have to start over from scratch. Write your next app in one language, and build it for both Android and iOS. Deliver the native look, feel, and performance you and your users expect from an app written with each platform's own tools and languages. Deliver apps fast, doing half the work you were doing before and exploiting powerful new features to speed up development. Write once, run anywhere.

Carmine Zaccagnino
(368 pages) ISBN: 9781680506952. $47.95
https://pragprog.com/book/czflutr

The Pragmatic Bookshelf

The Pragmatic Bookshelf features books written by professional developers for professional developers. The titles continue the well-known Pragmatic Programmer style and continue to garner awards and rave reviews. As development gets more and more difficult, the Pragmatic Programmers will be there with more titles and products to help you stay on top of your game.

Visit Us Online

This Book's Home Page
https://pragprog.com/book/dhios
Source code from this book, errata, and other resources. Come give us feedback, too!

Keep Up to Date
https://pragprog.com
Join our announcement mailing list (low volume) or follow us on twitter @pragprog for new titles, sales, coupons, hot tips, and more.

New and Noteworthy
https://pragprog.com/news
Check out the latest pragmatic developments, new titles and other offerings.

Save on the ebook

Save on the ebook versions of this title. Owning the paper version of this book entitles you to purchase the electronic versions at a terrific discount.

PDFs are great for carrying around on your laptop—they are hyperlinked, have color, and are fully searchable. Most titles are also available for the iPhone and iPod touch, Amazon Kindle, and other popular e-book readers.

Send a copy of your receipt to support@pragprog.com and we'll provide you with a discount coupon.

Contact Us

Online Orders:	*https://pragprog.com/catalog*
Customer Service:	*support@pragprog.com*
International Rights:	*translations@pragprog.com*
Academic Use:	*academic@pragprog.com*
Write for Us:	*http://write-for-us.pragprog.com*
Or Call:	+1 800-699-7764

Lightning Source UK Ltd.
Milton Keynes UK
UKHW031227100221
378555UK00006B/203